THE ARTHRITIS CURE FOR PETS

also by Brenda Adderly, M.H.A.

THE ARTHRITIS CURE FOR PETS

Brian Beale, D.V.M., D.A.C.V.S.,

and Brenda Adderly, M.H.A.

LITTLE, BROWN AND COMPANY

BOSTON NEW YORK LONDON

First Edition

Library of Congress Cataloging-in-Publication Data

Beale, Brian.
The arthritis cure for pets / Brian Beale & Brenda Adderly—1st ed.
p.   cm.
ISBN 0-316-08590-1
1. Dogs—Diseases—Alternative treatment.   2. Cats—Diseases—Alternative treatment.
3. Pets—Diseases—Alternative treatment.   4. Arthritis in animals—Alternative treatment.
I. Adderly, Brenda.   II. Title.

SF992.A77 B43 2000
636.7'0896722—dc21   99-049872

10   9   8   7   6   5   4   3   2   1

Q-FG

Book Design by Fearn Cutler de Vicq

Printed in the United States of America

To my wife, Karin; my son, Jared; my daughter, Danielle; and the hundreds of arthritic dogs and cats I have had the pleasure of working with over the years.

Brian Beale

This book is dedicated to our four-legged friends who are suffering with arthritis — hope *and* help are now on the way!

Brenda Adderly

Contents

ACKNOWLEDGMENTS

We'd like to acknowledge Jennifer Josephy, who is not only an accomplished editor but a real publishing professional and a great person to work with.

Several others made important contributions to this book — so we'd like to thank:

    Emma Beeler, D.V.M., Hermosa Animal Hospital,
        Hermosa Beach, CA
    Mari Florence, Backbone Books
    Gayle Grasmehr, D.V.M., Tarzana Pet Clinic, Tarzana, CA
    Debra Hoffman, D.V.M., Tarzana Pet Clinic, Tarzana, CA

And a hearty thank you to Marie Moneysmith for making it all work!

THE ARTHRITIS CURE FOR PETS

What Is Arthritis?

When she was growing up, Janna wanted a dog more than anything else. But every time she asked her parents for a puppy, they made excuses ranging from "We can't get a dog because we're going on vacation next month" to "What if you get tired of it and we end up taking care of it?" When she tried to convince them that having a dog was a good idea and that she would never get tired of it, they came up with new excuses. After a few years Janna suspected that she would probably never talk them into it. But she never gave up trying.

Not surprisingly, when Janna graduated from college, she went to the animal shelter and took home a small, fluffy black-and-white, mixed-breed puppy. Jack, as she called him, grew up to be an adorable little terrier-type dog with the personality of a clown. He chased everything, from the belt on Janna's bathrobe to butterflies and balls. Whenever she sat on the sofa to read a book or watch television, he climbed up next to her and curled up in her lap. At night Jack snuggled under Janna's comforter, then licked her toes in the morning when it was time for his walk. If that didn't work, Jack tugged at the comforter until he pulled it off the bed and Janna had no choice but to get up.

The first thing Janna learned about dogs from Jack was that her parents were right — they were a responsibility, much more like having a child than she imagined. Jack couldn't be left alone for more than seven or eight hours, meaning Janna's social life revolved around his feeding schedule and bathroom needs. When she wanted to go on vacation, there was always the question of what to do with him. He needed training, grooming, occasional trips to the veterinarian, flea treatments, toys — sometimes the list of things Janna did for Jack seemed longer than her own "to do" list.

But in spite of it all, Janna loved Jack with all her heart. In fact, the second thing he taught her was that a dog really is a best friend — an uncomplaining, uncritical, "always there for you" buddy. During the next seven years Jack helped Janna get through graduate school, one horrible job, two moves, a divorce, and her father's death. No matter what happened, Janna knew she could curl up with Jack and feel better just knowing he was there.

Eventually, though, Janna noticed that Jack's back legs seemed a little stiff in the morning. The veterinarian suspected that Jack might have arthritis in his hips or back. But when Janna asked about medication or treatments, the veterinarian shrugged off her question, saying, "Sooner or later, most dogs have problems like this. Jack is getting older and slowing down. He won't be around forever, you know."

Crushed, Janna left the veterinarian's office feeling helpless and lost. Her best friend was suffering and there was *nothing she could do about it — except watch and wait. Somehow it didn't seem fair. When she told her neighbor what was happening, the reply was "Well, he's only a dog." But Janna didn't see it quite that way. The following week she made some calls, found a veterinarian who specialized in treating arthritis, and drove an hour and a half each way to get a second opinion. Fortunately, this time the news was better. The new veterinarian told Janna that arthritis was no longer "the beginning of the end." In fact, there were plenty of options for her and Jack. And before long Janna was delighted to find Jack not only tugging at the comforter once again but also chasing his favorite ball with the same craziness he'd had as a puppy. "To think that he might have suffered needlessly if I hadn't gone for another opinion is really scary," she told her mother, who ended up being as charmed by the little dog as her daughter was. "I wish more people knew their dogs could have good lives — even if they have arthritis."*

Ten years ago Janna might not have been able to make Jack's golden years quite so golden. For humans and animals alike, a diagnosis of arthritis meant life would never be the same. Often it was easy to see why. Many people have experienced the devastating effects of the disease, either firsthand or with an older friend, relative, or beloved pet whose joints grew stiff or swollen, making even simple movements painful.

No one likes to see others suffer, but watching an animal's health decline can be especially hard to bear. Human beings are at least able to tell the doctor where it hurts and communicate the results of various treatments. But since animals can't communicate as humans do, there is a great deal of guesswork involved with animals that are sick, making it difficult to tell what is working and what is not.

The fact that we love our pets only complicates matters further. When a beloved dog, cat, or other animal that occupies a special place in our hearts is ill, emotions can overrule logic, making choices and decisions almost as hard as watching the pet suffer with early-onset or age-related arthritis.

•   •   •

Of the 59 million cats and 54 million dogs currently living in America, up to 25 percent, or one out of four, are likely to develop osteoarthritis before the end of their lives. *Millions of them are in pain right now.* And most veterinarians provide only temporary treatments — painkillers, such as nonsteroidal anti-inflammatory drugs (NSAIDs), and analgesics in mild cases; steroids or even surgery in more painful ones. These methods may alleviate the pain temporarily, but they treat only the symptoms, not the disease.

Fortunately, for a growing number of American veterinarians — and quite a few in Europe as well — the solution to osteoarthritis is different: they treat the symptoms *and* the disease. This type of therapy is a recent development and not yet widely recognized. But the bottom line is that osteoarthritis in cats, dogs, horses, and other animals can be halted, reversed, and often even cured. This book explains how.

With new scientific and technological breakthroughs, arthritis doesn't have to be a debilitating illness — for you or your best friend. Today there are a number of ways to ease the pain and other symptoms associated with arthritis. But the best way to understand the treatment is to understand the disease.

Arthritis Defined

There are actually more than a hundred different diseases falling under the umbrella term *arthritis*. Some of them, like rheumatoid arthritis, are familiar to most of us, while others, such as systemic lupus erythematosus, are not as well known. In many respects these various diseases are quite different from one another. What they all have in common, however, are symptoms involving pain and inflammation of the joints.

Rheumatoid arthritis, for example, is an autoimmune disease that involves severe chronic inflammation of the membranes surrounding the ends of the bones at the joints. The cause of rheumatoid arthritis is not known, but experts suspect that it is related to an immune system gone awry. Unlike osteoarthritis, rheumatoid arthritis is systemic, meaning it can spread throughout the body, with inflammation developing in other tissues, such as skin, muscles, blood vessels, and even the lungs and heart. It can cause tenderness, pain, and swelling of certain joints, as well as generalized symptoms like achiness, fever, and anemia.

In both humans and animals, however, the most common form of arthritis is osteoarthritis. And as a number of clinical studies have shown, osteoarthritis in animals is very similar to that in humans. It is interesting to note that osteoarthritis appears to progress much faster in dogs than in humans. Substantial osteoarthritis may be seen as early as three to four weeks after an injury in dogs, whereas a similar injury in humans may take years to lead to comparable changes.

It is a slow, progressive condition involving the breakdown of cartilage, a cushionlike substance that covers the ends of bones where they come together to form joints. As the cartilage wears away, the bones begin rubbing against each other. In the initial stages, there may be no obvious symptoms. Later, stiffness, limping, or difficulty with normal movements may occur. As the disease progresses, pain invariably develops. In many instances the pain is mild, but it can become excruciating, causing people and animals to avoid movement whenever possible. Osteoarthritis is a chronic condition, which means it is a long-term disease, even though the symptoms do not necessarily become worse over time.

> **Osteoarthritis can develop anywhere in an animal's body, in one or more joints. However, those most commonly affected are the hips and leg joints.**

The word *osteoarthritis* is a combination of the Greek word *osteo,* meaning "of the bone," and *arthro,* "joint." The word ending *itis* means that inflammation is involved, although many osteoarthritis sufferers have little or no inflammation.

This is not to say that an animal with osteoarthritis will never experience inflammation. After all, it is a normal result of the body's protection-and-repair process when faced with injury or disease, and even low-grade inflammation causes pain and irritation. To make matters worse, instead of diminishing when tissue repairs begin, inflammation can continue and get out of control, causing further tissue damage. Destructive enzymes are then released, encouraging a progressive, gradual degeneration of bone, cartilage, and surrounding tissues.

But with or without inflammation, osteoarthritis is painful, simply because the bones in the afflicted joints are losing their cushioning. When arthritis exists without inflammation, more accurate terms for the condition are *arthrosis* or *osteoarthrosis,* meaning "degenerative joint disease." In fact, veterinarians often prefer to use these terms for osteoarthritis, because they are more precise. You may find the disease referred to by these and other names, so it is useful to be aware of them. Such terms include the following:

- *Osteoarthrosis:* As mentioned above, this means a disease or condition involving physical changes around the joint. This definition is often more accurate, because it does not suggest inflammation.
- *Degenerative joint disease:* DJD is a disease caused by the degeneration of a component of the joint, such as the breakdown of cartilage. Some veterinarians like to use this term because, as in the case of osteoarthrosis, it does not imply that inflammation is occurring.

> In common conversation, the word *osteoarthritis*, accurate or not, is generally used.

- *Hypertrophic arthritis:* The word *hypertrophic* refers to extra growth. In this form of the disease, there is growth of excess bone or bone spurs on the joints.

Joints That Can Be Affected by Arthritis

When osteoarthritis progresses through the body, it does so asymmetrically and in no particular order. So, for example, only one of an animal's knees may be affected initially. Eventually, however, pairs of joints can become disabled. Weight-bearing joints, like the hips, knees, and ankles, are particularly susceptible.

Hip dysplasia: Ideally, the hip joint consists of a cup-shaped socket and a round ball-type bone that fit snugly together. But in the condition known as hip dysplasia, the joint is mal-formed, so the ball and socket do not fit as neatly as they should. As a result, the joint is unstable, allowing excess move-ment of the bones, which leads to calcium deposits, chronic inflammation, muscle pain in the legs, and breakdown of the hip socket tissues.

Hip dysplasia is an inherited condition that is commonly seen. Although no dog is immune to hip dysplasia, large pure-bred dogs are especially prone to it and have a more difficult time dealing with it because of their size. Although dysplasia is not evident in puppies, it can often be seen in radiographs when a dog is four to six months old. Because this is a congenital condition, dogs that have this problem should not be bred, since they will pass the trait on to their offspring.

Ligament tears in the knee (stifle) joint: The most common cause of arthritis in the knee is a tear of a ligament of the knee, called the anterior cruciate ligament, which makes the joint unstable.

Dislocation of the kneecap: In this condition, abnormally formed leg bones allow the kneecap to suddenly pop out of its proper position and slide back and forth. Chronic, low-grade inflam-mation develops from the repeated stress to the joint. This is an inherited condition often seen in smaller breeds of dogs from puppy mills or other poor breeding situations.

Arthritis of the hock or popping hock (ankle) joints: Arthritis of this joint can occur following trauma, such as a severely sprained ankle, or from development of bone chips due to osteochondrosis. It is one of the less common places in an animal's body for arthritis. (See Chapter 2 for a detailed explanation.)

Degeneration of the shoulder joint: The breakdown of cartilage in shoulder joints, as well as difficulties with the elbow (see below), may be due to trauma, joint instability, or osteochondrosis. Osteochondrosis is associated with poor breeding, inadequate diet, or a combination of the two. As the cartilage deteriorates, joint tissues become inflamed and painful. Arthritis of the shoulder is most frequently seen in larger dogs but may occur in small dogs as well.

Arthritis of the elbow: A hereditary condition common to larger breeds, this form of elbow dysplasia is similar to hip dysplasia, since it is also a result of malformed bones. As it develops, arthritis of the elbow and bone chips develop within the joint, causing pain and chronic lameness.

Arthritis of the wrist (carpi): Arthritis frequently occurs in this joint in animals that jump, either from high spots to the ground or vice versa, such as dogs who take a flying leap to catch a ball or Frisbee.

How to Make a Healthy Joint

In order to understand the causes, symptoms, and treatment of osteoarthritis in animals, it is important to have a general idea of how a healthy joint is structured and how it functions. All your pet's movements, from sitting to jumping on the bed to playing with you or another dog, depend on the precise and coordinated movement of joints. Although we tend to take such flexibility and movement for granted, when joints become injured or inflamed, this delicate and amazing interplay of moving parts is more fully appreciated.

Although humans and other mammals have certain similarities in their skeletal structure, the most obvious difference is that most animals are four-footed, which means their weight is more broadly distributed among the joints. This may be a gift of Mother Nature, since it allows lame animals to continue to move about more easily than a two-legged human with a similar problem.

That difference aside, animal joints are made up of the same basic elements that are found in humans: cartilage, joint capsules, the synovium, ligaments, tendons, muscles, and bursae.

Cartilage: A glistening, bluish white, spongy substance, *articular cartilage* — the medical term for the kind of cartilage found in joints — covers the ends of bones. Cartilage consists primarily of water, sugars, proteins called proteoglycans, and a tough, fibrous substance called collagen.

The combination of these substances makes healthy cartilage resilient enough to spring back into shape after it has been under pressure, such as when an animal is running. In a healthy joint, the spongy cartilage cushions and protects the bones during activity, serving as a "shock absorber" while providing a smooth, friction-free surface that enables the joint to move properly. When cartilage is in its prime, this surface is so smooth that it is actually more slippery than ice!

Cartilage is highly absorbent, and it is this feature that helps it remain healthy by soaking up nutritious synovial (see below) fluid that fills the joint space. A fine example of an incredibly efficient design, cartilage fills and empties itself of this fluid through normal joint movement. In this way, it is able to take in nutrients and cleanse itself of waste products as the animal goes through the normal motions of everyday life.

Joint capsule: At the ends of a bone, there is an area known as the subchondral bone, where the cartilage is attached. The subchondral bone and cartilage are both encased in a sealed capsule, called the joint capsule, or synovial sac. The joint capsule is made up of a tough, fibrous outer layer and a smooth, pliable inner layer, called the synovial membrane. The outside of the capsule consists of thick, cordlike fibers called ligaments. These are anchored to the bone on either side of the joint, where they help to keep the joint stable and hold the bones in correct alignment.

Muscles control joint movement and are attached to the joint bones by tendons, which are tough, dense cords of connective tissue that transmit the force of muscle exertion.

Synovial membrane: The lining inside the joint capsule is the thin, velvety smooth synovial membrane. Only one or two cells thick in a healthy joint, the membrane contains plentiful blood vessels and nerve endings, and produces a clear, viscous fluid resembling raw egg white that fills the capsule. The synovial fluid lubricates the joints and nourishes the cartilage, which has no blood vessels, and therefore no source of nutrients of its own.

Bursae: Lying outside the joint are small, fluid-filled sacs called bursae. These too produce a lubricating liquid and help protect the tendons and ligaments from injury.

Different Jobs for Different Joints

Because joints function in different ways, they are classified according to how they work and what they do.

Types of Joints

The skeleton is a dense, hard framework that protects delicate internal organs and supports muscle and skin. A joint, sometimes called an articulation, is the point at which two or more bones meet. Joints allow an animal to move in various directions and perform some very complicated activities. As a result, joints can be categorized by the degree of motion they allow, even though some do not allow any motion at all! The tough, fibrous joints in the skull known as sutures, for example, connect the various skull bones but are not designed for movement.

Other joints, like the pelvis, permit only limited movement. Then there are joints that permit a wide range of movement, such as those in the wrist, neck, and hip. The majority of joints in the body are of this type. Unfortunately, these are the joints most likely to develop osteoarthritis, although other types of joints can be affected as well. Joints are also grouped according to the direction in which they move. Some of the major types are

Gliding joint: This kind of joint allows a slight gliding movement. A good example is the joints in the spine, which give it flexibility. Cats are endowed with marvelous gliding joints that permit them to take those luxurious postnap stretches and arch their backs in that familiar Halloween pose.

Hinge joint: Like door hinges, these allow the digits of the paw, for instance, to open and close. Other examples are knee and elbow joints.

Ball-and-socket joint: The upper end of this joint is round, like a ball, and fits neatly into a cuplike socket. This unique joint allows movement in all directions. The prime example of this is the shoulder joint, the most freely moving joint in the entire body. Hip joints are also ball-and-socket joints.

Saddle joint: With one bone concave and the other convex, this joint resembles a saddle on a horse's back, or a pair of nesting spoons. Saddle joints, like those in the wrist and thumb, do not rotate. Instead, they move up and down and from side to side.

Another way to categorize joints is to distinguish them as weight-bearing or non-weight-bearing. The primary weight-bearing joints are the shoulders, elbows, wrists, ankles, knees, and hips. These are the joints that bear the full brunt of mechanical stress and are the ones most likely to show the results of wear-and-tear over time. An exception is the ankle, which is less commonly affected by osteoarthritis.

How Osteoarthritis Changes the Joints

As osteoarthritis develops, the fundamental change that occurs is a breakdown of cartilage at the site of the joint. Cartilage becomes softer and starts to lose its elasticity, and the surface can become worn or thin in spots. The cartilage slowly loses its ability to absorb sufficient supplies of synovial fluid to keep it healthy. As the cartilage deteriorates, there is less and less of it between the two bones that meet at the joint. Eventually the cartilage may become so thin that the bones rub together, and fissures, tiny pits, and cracks in the bones can develop. An animal's body attempts to repair the damage, often making the situation worse. The end of the bones may thicken, or bone spurs can form, creating bony enlargements around the joint. In addition, sometimes pieces of cartilage or bone break off and float in the joint fluid, irritating and inflaming the delicate synovial membrane lining the joint.

As osteoarthritis progresses, the animal's cartilage wears away. Joints become painful and stiff, making movement so difficult that it is sometimes avoided unless absolutely necessary. This tendency not to use an arthritic joint can make the problem worse by weakening the muscles and ligaments around the joint and making it even stiffer. In the last stages of arthritis, the cartilage may be completely worn away and the bone fully exposed.

The effects of osteoarthritis are not limited to the cartilage, however. The disease also affects tissues in and around the joints, including the subchondral bone, the joint capsule, and the muscles surrounding the joint.

Dispelling the Myths

Why do these changes occur? What happens within the body that makes some — but not all — animals develop osteoarthritis? Over the years a number of theories have been advanced, many of which have turned out to be inaccurate. For example, there is a common assumption that age-related arthritis in animals is an inevitable consequence of growing older. Even many veterinarians believe that most animals are doomed to develop the disease and end their lives as frail, pain-ridden, decrepit shadows of their former selves.

Fortunately, this point of view is quickly being replaced by recent medical and technological developments in diagnosing and treating osteoarthritis. As a result, many animals now lead long, healthy lives in spite of arthritis.

Among the many misconceptions about osteoarthritis is the long-held belief that joints become stiff and painful because of wear-and-tear caused by normal, everyday activity. In fact, this theory underlies the traditional medical opinion that says there is nothing much that can be done about osteoarthritis in your pet, since once cartilage has deteriorated, it is gone forever.

But in the early 1980s several articles appeared documenting evidence of cartilage regeneration. These findings caused a fundamental shift in the way osteoarthritis is viewed. In fact, a recent article in the *Journal of the American Medical Association* acknowledged the popularity, as well as the effectiveness, of nutritional therapies. "There may well be biological mechanisms by which some nutraceuticals influence processes in OA [osteoarthritis]," said Dr. Timothy McAlindon of the Boston University School of Medicine. "Both glucosamine and chondroitin sulfate resemble molecules present in cartilage, suggesting that these substances could provide substrate for repair of cartilage damaged in OA."[1]

Then on January 13, 1997, Jane Brody, the *New York Times* health columnist, reported on her experience with giving two supplements, glucosamine and chondroitin sulfate, to her dog:

Fourteen months ago, following my arthritic spaniel's dramatic improvement upon taking a supplement containing two substances that play a role in the formation of cartilage, glucosamine and chondroitin sulfate, I decided to try the stuff myself. . . . Now a year later my dog and I are still taking the supplement, though at lower daily doses. My dog, who will be 13 in June, is free of pain and stiffness. He walks two hours a day, goes up and down stairs easily and regularly climbs a mountain road with me.

The March 8, 1998, broadcast of *Dateline NBC* devoted a full segment to Jane Brody and her dog, totally mobile and, in all visible respects, fully cured of the disease.

Exercise and Osteoarthritis

In addition to changes on the cellular level, the correlation between exercise and symptoms of osteoarthritis has also been studied. Again, the wear-and-tear theory was found to be outdated. The most important finding is that moderate, consistent exercise does not promote osteoarthritis. In fact, such activity improves the functioning of an animal's joints by strengthening surrounding muscles and stabilizing the joint. As a result, the cartilage is less likely to be harmed during everyday activity or exercise.

There are two exceptions. The first involves a joint that has been injured — if an animal has been hit by a car, for example. The second is the result of repetitive impact loading, like repeatedly taking a horse over fences or playing long sessions of Frisbee catch with a dog. These types of joint injuries or abuse can lead to "secondary" arthritis, in which a specific event or frequent repetition of a particular activity is the primary cause. Obesity can also bring on secondary arthritis, simply because the excess weight puts additional pressure on the joints and cartilage. But regular, moderate exercise is now accepted as a means of improving arthritis symptoms, rather than making them worse.

In fact, several studies have specifically examined the effect of jogging on the risk of developing osteoarthritis. Researchers have found that far from damaging joints, regular jogging in middle age is likely to help maintain physical function. Only among long-distance runners did there seem to be an increased risk of developing osteoarthritis in the knee and hip.

Other recent investigations, including one at the University of Iowa College of Medicine, have demonstrated that lifelong moderate — and probably even strenuous — joint use does not cause cartilage degeneration in normal animal joints with proper alignment, stability, articular surfaces, innervation, and muscle control.[2]

Interestingly, in the Iowa study the researchers noted that a lack of "loading or static loading activity"— in other words, inactivity — produced more degeneration of the cartilage "matrix," the area where cartilage is created, and could eventually lead to loss of joint function. What this means to a pet owner is that an animal that spends long days housebound or sleeping appears to be at greater risk of developing osteoarthritis than a pet that is regularly taken for walks or engages in play during its waking hours.

In a study of osteoarthritis in humans, researchers have concluded that lifelong moderate use of normal, healthy joints does not increase the risk of cartilage degeneration. In other words, osteoarthritis is not the result of aging, although, as the authors state, there is a strong correlation between increased age and the prevalence of the disease.[3]

The same authors are quick to point out, however, that repeated high-impact activities and torsional loading (movements that twist or wrench the joints, such as the fast turns made by many herding dogs) can damage normal joints. Furthermore, joints are more susceptible to arthritis when they are not correctly formed or are unstable, when they receive inadequate support because nearby muscles are weak, or when the joint or muscle nerves are not functioning properly.

Consequently, it is important to realize that even young dogs can develop osteoarthritis from repetitive jumping or overexertion. Good examples are dogs that jump high into the air when playing catch. The wear-and-tear on joints and muscles from jumping several times the animal's body height and then landing, especially on hard surfaces, can sometimes cause premature deterioration. One recent study shows a slight increased risk of developing osteoarthritis in weight-bearing joints when there is *very frequent and heavy exercise over many years*. For the majority of less active dogs, however, routine recreational physical activity neither decreases nor increases the risk of developing arthritis.[4]

Understand, though, that the debate over the consequences of exercise on joints is not over yet. Researchers at the University of Kuopio, in Finland, examined the effects of running in a controlled study of mice. Those mice in the runner group exercised daily from the age of two months to eighteen months, and were sacrificed at intervals within this period. Examination of the knee joints in the runners, as compared with mice in the control group, which did not exercise, showed that moderate, long-lasting running accelerates the development of osteoarthritis in the knee joints. Even so, no one knows yet if these findings apply only to mice or to mammals in general.

The New Thinking: Osteoarthritis Begins in the Cells

While we wait for the final word on whether physical stress is a factor in the development of osteoarthritis, scientists can say for certain that the origins of the disease are rooted in metabolic changes in the cartilage itself. The progressive deterioration of joints occurs when chondrocytes, special cells in the cartilage that create new collagen and other cartilage ingredients, go awry. When this happens, the chondrocytes produce cartilage-destroying enzymes, like metalloproteinases, as well as nitric oxide. Nitric oxide not only causes oxidative damage to tissue but also contributes to a process called apoptosis, which kills chondrocyte cells. As a result, existing cartilage degenerates faster than new cartilage can be produced. Antioxidant vitamins and nitric oxide inhibitors are being studied as means of fighting this aspect of the disease. Meanwhile, other experts are approaching treatment from the opposite perspective, by examining ways of creating more cartilage. For reasons that are not yet clear, changes in the tissue and cell chemistry cause existing cartilage to degenerate faster than new cartilage can be produced.

At the Department of Veterinary Pathology and Department of Veterinary Clinical Science and Animal Husbandry at the University of Liverpool, researchers conducted a study of how cartilage changes with osteoarthritis. Cartilage from seven dogs with osteoarthritis was compared with healthy cartilage from five other dogs. Researchers examined a substance called type VI collagen, which is an essential element in the cartilage matrix. In healthy cartilage, the type VI collagen was concentrated in the capsule next to chondrocytes. In the osteoarthritic cartilage, however, researchers found that this form of collagen was present throughout the cartilage matrix and was greatly increased in the region surrounding chondrocytes.[5]

As the study authors point out, here is evidence that cartilage can regenerate. The higher concentration of type VI collagen in the chondrocyte area, where cartilage production takes place, is a sign that the body's own natural healing process is under way.

Researchers have concluded that these collagen fibers, which organize and stabilize other major collagen fibers, are part of an active process designed to repair damaged osteoarthritic cartilage.[6]

Other studies also provide evidence of cartilage regeneration and repair. In one study that explored this process, scientists examined osteoarthritic cartilage and found primitive forms of proteoglycans, large molecules made up of protein and sugars that are one of the essential ingredients of cartilage. This primitive proteoglycan is typically found in immature cartilage. From this discovery, the researchers concluded that the healing process occurring in articular cartilage is similar to the process that takes place in other damaged connective tissue, such as skin and tendons. This immature cartilage appears soon after injury and throughout the mending process, thereby supporting the theory that the body produces it specifically as a means of repairing cartilage.

These same researchers also report that in dogs, osteoarthritis increases collagen synthesis. But unlike the proteoglycans production, the collagen is not a primitive form, but a mature version primarily responsible for cartilage growth.

With this growing body of evidence to support cartilage regeneration, the wear-and-tear theory of osteoarthritis is definitely on the wane. So too is the notion that osteoarthritis is inevitable and that once a beloved pet develops this condition, there is nothing that can be done.

The new understanding of osteoarthritis has also opened up the possibility of new avenues of healing. One focus is on how healthy cartilage may be affected by three major factors — heredity, poor nutrition, and injury. Subsequent chapters look at each of these points in greater detail.

Other researchers are also finding ways to repair and maintain normal cartilage structure and function, for instance, healing with supplements of glucosamine and chondroitin sulfate.

Studies from around the world amply demonstrate the potential of these supplements when it comes to osteoarthritis. Clinical research from Europe, South America, and Asia has demonstrated the healing value of glucosamine and chondroitin sulfate in people. In years past, public acceptance of such treatments would have been difficult without widespread support from veterinarians. Today strides in the treatment of osteoarthritis in animals are being made in the United States, where research and clinical reports attest to the benefits of glucosamine and purified chondroitin sulfate. Progressive veterinarians herald glucosamine and chondroitin as the wave of the future, and success stories are everywhere, from pet magazines to the Internet.

New Medical Procedures for Treating Osteoarthritis

Before discussing the amazing ability of glucosamine and chondroitin sulfate to promote cartilage mending and to reverse osteoarthritis, let's take a look at some of the other accepted methods of regenerating cartilage. Physicians are currently using some, and researchers continue to experiment with others. Any decision to use these options for your pet should be made with advice from your veterinarian, who can inform you of the short- and long-term benefits and concerns associated with any treatment protocol.

Pharmaceutical Medications

Although it began as a treatment for show and racehorses with orthopedic problems, Adequan, from Luitpold Pharmaceuticals in Shirley, New York, can alleviate arthritis and hip dysplasia pain in dogs too. In addition, studies have shown that it also promotes cartilage healing. Keep in mind, though, that it works best in mild to moderate situations. In advanced stages of the disease, Adequan may not provide enough pain relief to make a difference.

> **Adequan has been approved in the United States for use by veterinarians on dogs and horses suffering from osteoarthritis.**

Derived from the tracheae and lungs of cows, Adequan is purified glycosaminoglycan (GAG) polysulfate, part of a family of molecules that serve as precursors in the creation of joint fluid and cartilage. Adequan treatments can enhance the quality of the joint fluid, as well as protect and repair cartilage.

The medication is fairly costly and requires several trips to the veterinarian, since it must be injected into the muscle once or twice a week for anywhere from one to eight weeks. Once the pet improves, monthly maintenance visits are recommended. Side effects are rare.

Rimadyl is a nonsteroidal anti-inflammatory drug that was created especially for relieving pain and inflammation in dogs. Studies have shown that it does provide relief for osteoarthritis symptoms. Although Rimadyl was introduced only in 1997, it is one of the top ten bestselling products in the U.S. animal-health market, with more than 1 million dogs now on the medication. Rimadyl has fewer side effects than other anti-inflammatory drugs, but on rare occasions it can cause digestive upset or liver problems. If your dog takes Rimadyl, follow-up visits to the veterinarian are recommended.

Cartilage Transplantation

In recent years considerable progress has been made with this technique. In animal studies, for example, bone and cartilage cells have been successfully transplanted from one mouse to another.

In humans the technique is known as autologous chondro-cyte implantation (ACI) and involves healthy living cartilage that is removed from the patient and used to cultivate a living graft. This graft is then implanted into the damaged, arthritic joint. ACI has proved useful in healing secondary arthritis resulting from injuries, but not primary arthritis.

This technique is also being performed on dogs and horses but is currently in the experimental stage. It is too early to tell whether this alternative form of cartilage can withstand the pressures of normal use.

Scientists have high hopes for a related procedure (being studied at New York's Beth Israel Hospital) that involves removing a portion of cartilage from an inflamed joint and then cloning it in a laboratory. The new growth is reinjected into the joint to stimulate the creation of new cartilage. Although it is expensive now, this technique may be affordable for the average patient someday.

Test tube cartilage: In the laboratories of the Massachusetts Institute of Technology (MIT), scientists are experimenting with growing cartilage in test tubes. Thus far, they have produced a substance that is stiff but flexible and nearly the same as human cartilage. But it is too early to say whether this material can be transplanted into joints to repair cartilage damage associated with arthritis.

Chondrogeneron: This is a combination of fibrinogen, a simple protein commonly found in animal tissues, and a cartilage-regenerating substance called transforming growth factor beta

(TGFβ). When used together, the fibrinogen helps the TGFβ adhere to the injured cartilage. Chondrogeneron may one day be used to treat osteoarthritis in pets, since it has been used successfully to repair cartilage and promote cartilage growth in laboratory animals.

Meniscus transplants: The meniscus is a type of fibrous cartilage found in the knee joint. Experiments are under way in America to use donated meniscal tissue or synthetic material to restore a damaged meniscus. But more studies are needed before this procedure can be considered viable for human or animal osteoarthritis.

Hope Has Arrived

The good news is that your animal no longer has to suffer needlessly from the pain and debilitation of arthritis. If you're reading this book, you're obviously concerned about your pet's health and the possibilities for treating osteoarthritis. Damaged cartilage can be repaired and the degenerative process of osteoarthritis reversed. Chapter 4 takes a closer look at the wonders of glucosamine and chondroitin sulfate, and offers stories that will warm your heart and give you and your pet hope.

• • •

Now, let's take a more in-depth look at the disease in animals, including its causes, signs, and symptoms.

Arthritis and Your Pet

According to fossil records, the human-dog relationship is an ancient one, going back roughly fourteen thousand years — to the Stone Age, or Paleolithic, period. Therefore, man and dog were partners about four thousand years before mankind had developed agriculture. Some experts speculate that perhaps these first dogs were hunting partners, helping their human companions track and chase food. Others present a less appealing scenario, postulating that the dogs themselves were kept as a food source for when game was scarce. Some combination of the two theories is probably closest to the truth.

The Same — and Different

While that mystery remains unsolved, we do know that the human-dog bond is a particularly strong one. Humans have revered and idolized cats — as well as feared and even exterminated them — and horses have been prized, displayed, and traded for centuries. But when it comes to companionship, dogs and humans have a natural affinity for each other. Considering the similarities between the two species, it is not surprising. After all, both dogs and humans are social animals, living in "packs" with one member considered the leader. And yet at the same time, both humans and dogs can be very protective and territorial. We also have common elements in our body language, expressions, and responses to certain situations, like joy at seeing a familiar face and shame when scolded.

Scientists generally agree that all the dogs in existence today are descendants of the wolf. During the hundreds of years that followed those first early associations, humans inadvertently became involved in dog breeding by selecting to live with those that best served their needs. So, for example, one community might value large dogs that were capable of pulling or carrying loads. Another group might befriend only dogs that barked when strangers approached, or those animals that were particularly fine and swift hunters.

More recently humans have become much more involved in dog breeding, carefully selecting specific traits that are often not so much for practical purposes as for aesthetics. As a result, we now have dogs with black-and-white spotted coats, for example, or very small versions of standard dogs, such as toy poodles. Although there seems to be a purebred dog for almost every human preference, the selective breeding process also produced unforeseen results. In many breeds, careless practices, like inbreeding, have created genetic abnormalities, including predisposition to blindness or hearing loss, hip dysplasia, and other illnesses. In addition, breeding for specific physical traits has led to health problems: the long, low body of a dachshund tends to develop spinal difficulties.

In spite of the observable differences in various breeds, however, all dogs share the same physiology. Other than size, there are no real differences between the bodies of a four-pound Chihuahua, for instance, and a 220-pound mastiff. Even more amazing is that, except for the lack of a collarbone, dogs and humans have the same musculoskeletal system, although dogs' front legs are more highly developed than our arms because they carry half the animal's weight.

In addition, there are many similarities between humans and dogs when it comes to the cardiovascular, nervous, endocrine, urinary, reproductive, and respiratory systems. The primary differences between humans and their best friends lie in the areas of the digestive system, skin and hair, and the senses, especially hearing, smell, and sight. Dogs, for example, do not need to chew food and mix it with saliva in order to digest it, since that entire process is done in the stomach. And unlike humans, dogs

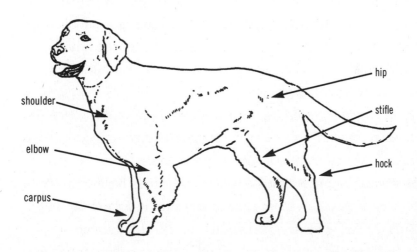

do not cool their bodies by perspiring through their skin. Instead, excess heat passes only through the pads of their feet or from the mouth and tongue during panting.

Even though dogs are equipped with the same elements as humans in their eyes and ears, both senses operate very differently in the canine version. Dim light, for example, does not impede a dog's vision as much as it does a human's, but they recognize fewer colors than people do. Similarly, a dog's hearing is about twice as sharp as a human's is. In fact, the only sense more highly developed in dogs than hearing is smell, which is a whopping one hundred times more powerful than human olfactory ability.

Our Common Enemy

There is one other thing that humans and dogs both have in common, and its effect on both species began long before the two began living together. Osteoarthritis has been with us — and with the canine species — for eons, showing up in human skeletons half a million years old. Treatments date back almost as far. Thousands of years ago, arthritis sufferers sought out the heat of early health spas, such as the Roman baths, and mineral waters to ease their aches and pains.

As we have seen, any creature with a bony skeleton can develop osteoarthritis — reptiles, birds, and amphibians, as well as underwater mammals, like porpoises and whales. But perhaps most astonishing is that signs of osteoarthritis have been identified in the bones of those ancient creatures known today only by their skeletal remains, the dinosaurs of 150 million years ago. It is very likely that even some of the earth's earliest inhabitants roamed the land with an arthritic limp!

Today, osteoarthritis is one of the most common problems that bring pet owners to veterinarians for counsel and treatment.

Dogs, horses, and to a lesser degree cats can develop this disabling disease at any age, whether they are purebreds or mixed breeds. Arthritis is also more common in large-breed dogs than in small-breed dogs and cats simply because large animals' joints have to carry more weight.

According to a study published in the journal *Veterinary Clinics of North America: Small Animal Practice* in 1997, 24 percent of dogs being treated at "multi-center referral canine practices" were seen for musculoskeletal disorders, and 70 percent of those cases involved difficulties with bones in the limbs. Even in dogs younger than one year old, 22 percent of the cases involved this type of problem.[7]

Popular breeds of dogs are more prone to the disease, very likely because these breeds are often raised in "puppy mills," where in-breeding (mating animals that are closely related or that have similar genetics) increases the risk of developing osteoarthritis and a host of other congenital ailments. If you are interested in a purebred pet, do not make your selection impulsively. Do enough homework to ensure that you are getting an animal from a reliable, respected breeder.

The most common type of osteoarthritis in animals is secondary arthritis. As we have seen, this type of arthritis is the result of or related to (i.e., "secondary" to) a predisposing condition such as hip dysplasia, elbow dysplasia, torn ligaments, or diseases of the joints, like osteochondrosis. These conditions can occur in most breeds of dogs, but the larger ones, such as the rottweiler, Labrador retriever, golden retriever, and German shepherd, are more commonly affected.

The most common causes of osteoarthritis in small-dog breeds include torn ligaments (especially in the knee), kneecap dislocation, and Legg-Calve-Perthes disease, a condition found in small-breed dogs that involves degeneration of the head of the thighbone. Breeds often affected include the miniature poodle, bichon frise, shih tzu, beagle, and Yorkshire terrier.

A Quick Course in Cats

Cats' musculoskeletal systems are also very similar to humans'. They even have collarbones (clavicles), which dogs do not. But in addition, felines have approximately forty more bones than humans do. Although we both use tendons and ligaments for movement and have many bones in common, a cat's skeletal system accommodates the cat lifestyle. Whereas a dog's front legs — the equivalent of a human's arms — are sturdier than ours and bear more of the body's weight, in cats it is the rear legs that are more highly developed. This gives our feline friends their

unparalleled ability to leap and to move quickly. Another advantage found in the feline skeletal system is an extremely flexible spine, allowing cats greater freedom of movement than either humans or dogs.

Cats' bones and joints are similar to those in dogs and humans, but most of the joints are hinged. The only ball-and-socket joints in cats are in the shoulders and hips. The outer layer of their bones is called the cortex. A poor diet affects the cortex, leading to problems in bone development or brittle bones that fracture easily. Chapter 7 discusses in more detail the elements of a proper diet for cats.

Osteoarthritis in Cats

Although osteoarthritis in cats is considered a treatable disease, as we noted earlier, it occurs less frequently than in dogs, and is therefore less well documented. Cases of cats with this disability are usually included in review studies, but dogs are normally the primary focus of the research. Even when joint disease in cats is studied, the type usually addressed is one of the polyarthritis syndromes, involving inflammation of several joints, rather than osteoarthritis.[8]

According to Elizabeth M. Hardie, D.V.M., Ph.D., of the College of Veterinary Medicine at North Carolina State University, there are several reasons for the lack of data on the incidence of the disease in cats. First, cats have relatively small bodies, as well as a remarkable ability to adjust to orthopedic abnormalities. This flexibility lets them redistribute weight bearing to other limbs far more easily than a dog can.

In cats, the joints most commonly affected by arthritis are the shoulders and elbows, although Maine coon cats have a predisposition to hip dysplasia. But as Hardie points out, cats' agility can mask arthritic symptoms, making it difficult to tell if they are uncomfortable or having difficulty moving. In fact, cats may appear to have a normal gait even when there is mild to moderate joint pain.

Since it is a progressive condition, arthritis can be more easily diagnosed in older cats, simply because the symptoms are worse. For example, in a North Carolina State University study that involved analysis of X rays from sixty-eight older (over the age of twelve) feline patients, the presence of osteoarthritis was identified in 20 percent of the animals. Nine of the cats had arthritis in the elbow, three in the shoulder, one had arthritis of the hip, and one in the ankle. Eight of these cats had joint problems bilaterally, that is, if one shoulder was affected, the other was too.[9]

A Weighty Issue

Like humans, dogs and cats in this country are frequently overweight. An estimated 30 percent of the American human population is considered obese (generally defined as being about 30 percent over ideal weight), while anywhere from 25 to 60 percent of the nation's dogs and cats are estimated to be overweight. (It would be interesting to know whether the overweight humans and animals live in the same households, but there do not seem to be any studies in this area.) In fact, some veterinarians feel that obesity is the foremost nutritional problem among companion animals in this country, increasing the risk of arthritis as well as heart, kidney, and liver disease and diabetes.[10]

It is easy to see how this situation has developed. Health experts point to poor eating habits and lack of exercise as two leading causes of obesity in humans. And it is a safe bet that if a dog's owners spend their leisure time snacking on a couch in front of the television, then the dog is probably sedentary — and nibbling on junk food — too.

In some ways, it is a cozy scenario not really so different from that of our Stone Age ancestors, with man and beast sharing a meal in front of the twenty-first-century equivalent of an open fire. The problem is that neither man nor beast is designed to carry excess weight. The additional strain placed on the joints of an animal that is burdened by extra pounds affects the cartilage and joint health in general.

If you are uncertain whether your dog is overweight, keep in mind that they should have classic hourglass figures, with nipped waistlines. If your dog is fully grown and still has a "puppy tummy," he or she is probably overweight. Another way to determine a weight problem is by lining up both your thumbs with the dog's backbone and running your fingers down the rib cage toward the hind legs. Can you feel your dog's ribs without having to push through a thick layer of fat? If so, your dog is probably at a healthy weight. But if the ribs are difficult to feel, it's time to start a reducing program.

Changing a dog's diet and slowly increasing the amount of exercise your dog gets can help him or her shed those pounds. Your veterinarian can also recommend foods that are low in calories but supply enough nutrition to keep a dog healthy while losing weight. For a dog that does not have arthritis, losing weight is a good preventive measure. For a pet that is showing signs of the disease, less weight means less stress on the joints and, therefore, less pain. Chapter 7 takes a more in-depth look at the role of diet, and Chapter 9 deals with exercise.

The Dark Side of the Golden Years

Osteoarthritis can be particularly troublesome for older animals. For one thing, in aging pets the disease is more resistant to treatment. Even if the osteoarthritis is caught in time to prevent it from getting worse — and even if it improves — the pain, stiffness, and depression animals suffer as a result are likely to continue for some time. This is particularly true because many animals with arthritis compensate for their chronic pain by contorting their back, which tends to cramp the muscles and make the pain worse.

There is no way to avoid growing older. So until the fountain of youth is discovered, a smart pet owner will do everything possible to make an animal's transition to old age painless. Avoiding injury, maintaining healthy eating practices, exercising, and taking nutrients are all part of successful aging — for two- and four-legged animals alike. Chapter 11 discusses various strategies to help your pet age gracefully.

The Degrees of the Disease

One way for a pet owner to measure the severity of osteoarthritis is to compare the pet's symptoms with those that occur in each stage of its development.

For example, a dog with mild osteoarthritis might exhibit a loss of 10 to 20 percent of its range of motion, or ability to move. There may be a small amount of stiffness or lameness when walking, especially when the dog gets up in the morning or after strenuous exercise. Sometimes a dog will lick the joint that is most troublesome.

In the moderate stages of the disease, range of motion can decrease by anywhere from 20 to 50 percent. This may lead to a dog's hesitating or even refusing to jump into a car or go up and down stairs. In addition, it may take longer for the dog to rise when lying down, and it might prefer to sit rather than stand. Stiffness or lameness is more noticeable, and touching the arthritic joint may cause the dog to flinch or whimper.

When the disease has progressed to the point at which it is defined as severe, the dog may have great difficulty rising or walking more than a few steps at once. Whining or whimpering can become frequent, as can licking the sore joint. There can be very obvious behavioral changes, such as refusing to let anyone touch the affected area.

Keep in mind that the most important indicator that something is wrong with an animal's health is a change in behavior. Humans often become cranky and short-tempered when they do not feel well or are in pain, and the same is true of pets. But, again like humans, not all animals respond the same way to pain. Some may seem depressed and lethargic. Others become aggressive, even toward a beloved family member. And still others cry, groan, or whine when in pain.

Although dogs frequently exhibit lameness, the majority of cats do not. A cat with arthritis may lose weight or have accidents outside the litter box, simply because access to food or litter may have become difficult. Other cats behave aggressively when picked up, because of sore joints. Similarly, joint pain can prevent a cat from grooming itself thoroughly, resulting in uncharacteristic matting or unkempt fur.[11]

If you suspect that your pet has osteoarthritis, see a veterinarian. There are other conditions that could be causing the symptoms, and before beginning treatment, it is important to know for certain what you are treating.

Diagnosis should not be made on the appearance of X rays alone. There is no correlation between the level of pain and the extent of degeneration that shows up in X rays or even in physical examination. If a pet appears to be in pain or has a decreased level of activity that is thought to be due to osteoarthritis, conservative treatment should be started immediately and continued indefinitely.[12]

If the veterinarian does find evidence of arthritis, often the first and immediate line of defense is pain relievers. Remember, pain is a stressful experience for the entire body, and a pet should not be allowed to suffer unnecessarily.

Keep in mind that although dogs can sometimes tolerate pain relievers designed for humans, such as enteric-coated aspirin, these products can be lethal to cats. No matter what type of pain relievers you give your pet, there is a chance that they may cause serious stomach problems. You should watch for any signs of trouble with digestion or elimination, and consult your veterinarian if there are problems. In Chapter 5 you will learn about how the Arthritis Cure for Pets can be successfully integrated into a total treatment program for your pet.

Risk Factors and Causes of Osteoarthritis in Animals

The American veterinary community has only recently started to change its position on the cause of osteoarthritis. As already mentioned, it is no longer considered the inevitable result of everyday wear-and-tear from the normal use of joints. Recent research on the causes of osteoarthritis cites three primary factors as significantly increasing the risk of developing this disease: heredity, poor nutrition, and injury.

Heredity

Breeding Practices

Poor breeding practices increase the risk of osteoarthritis in animals by raising the genetic odds of developing predisposing conditions of the disease.

According to reports by the Humane Society of the United States, puppy mills — breeding facilities that are more interested in profits than in animals' health — are notorious for breeding animals that should not be bred, simply because they are likely to pass on hereditary problems to their offspring. This practice, coupled with risk factors such as inadequate diet, makes it more likely that a pet will develop arthritis. Responsible breeders who see early signs of arthritis in a purebred dog or cat may either not breed the animal or euthanize it to prevent later suffering or the chance that the animal may, in turn, pass the traits on to yet another generation.

Congenital Conditions

There are several congenital conditions (known as arthropathies) that may be present in young dogs which are known to lead to the development of degenerative joint disease. Many studies have found that abnormal bone anatomy can lead to a greater likelihood of developing arthritis. For example, the authors of one review have concluded that abnormal anatomy, disturbances in the nerve supply to a joint or muscle (innervation), joint instability, and inadequate muscle strength or endurance are all risk factors.[13] The following are several of the more common congenital defects that can contribute to osteoarthritis:

Canine hip dysplasia (CHD): This congenital condition is frequently a cause of secondary osteoarthritis and is the leading cause of lameness occurring in the rear legs of dogs. CHD is quite common in dogs, particularly in certain large and giant breeds, although smaller dogs and cats can suffer from the condition as well. Although it is usually an inherited trait, CHD can occur in puppies with normal parents. The development of the condition is due to other factors, including rapid growth rate, weight, and inappropriate nutrition.

Signs of CHD: Dogs are not born with CHD. The condition develops as the animal grows, although the resulting lameness can sometimes be seen in dogs as young as four months old; some dogs do not appear lame until later in life. CHD involves loose ligaments that fail to hold the round knob at the head of the thighbone (*femur*) in place in the hip socket or cup (*acetabulum*). The situation becomes worse if the cup itself is shallow and doesn't provide a deep resting place for the femur. The end result is a loose, unstable joint, in which the ball of the femur slides free of the hip socket. This laxity causes excessive wear on the cartilage in the hip joint, eventually resulting in arthritis.

Normally both hips are affected. When seen from behind, the dog's gait may appear to be stilted or there could be a "pelvic swing," greater on the side of the hip that is most affected. When the dog tries to change gait, from a trot to a run, it may appear to "bunny hop." When the dog stands, it may hunch its back to avoid extending the hips. There may also be stiffness on rising that improves as the dog moves around. Intense exercise usually makes the discomfort, lameness, and stiffness worse — especially the following day. Manipulation of the troubled hip, especially extension, will result in mild to moderate pain or discomfort. The muscles of the hind limb are often small due to underdevelopment or disease atrophy.

Traditional treatment ranges from easing symptoms using conservative management, such as pain relievers, weight reduction, and exercise, to hip-replacement surgery, which is very effective — although somewhat expensive.

Osteochondritis dissecans, or osteochondrosis (OCD): The origins of this condition are thought to be both genetic and environmental, but an exact cause has not been identified. OCD causes a thickening and growth of cartilage covering the head of a long bone, such as the humerus, running between the shoulder and elbow joints. The defective cartilage results in poor development of the subchondral bone directly beneath it. When weight-bearing activity applies pressure to the joint, the cartilage over the defective bone is traumatized and can develop fractures and fissures. Pieces of cartilage or bone may break off and become lodged in the joint space, causing lameness.

OCD can affect the following joints: the humeral head of the shoulder, the medial humeral condyle of the elbow, the lateral femoral condyle of the stifle joint, and the medial or lateral trochlear ridges of the ankle. In plain English, this means that the joints of the shoulder, elbow, stifle, and ankle are affected.

There are more than forty different medium- and giant-breed canines — specifically, those weighing over thirty-five pounds — that are most likely to develop OCD and, eventually, arthritis.

Signs of OCD: A gradual, mild to moderate lameness that gets worse with activity is the primary symptom of OCD and usually appears early, between the ages of four and twelve months. As many as 80 percent of all cases involve the same joint on the opposite limb. Other joints may be involved as well.

The animal is troubled by lameness in the more affected limb when the joint is flexed. When the joint is manipulated, the animal shows signs of discomfort. The recommended treatment is surgery soon after diagnosis, to reduce the effects of the underlying cause. These patients greatly benefit from glucosamine-chondroitin therapy after surgery.

Canine elbow dysplasia: More than fifty large- and giant-breed dogs are affected by elbow dysplasia, which is actually a collective category of various conditions. In recent years the incidence of these joint problems has risen, possibly because of poor breeding practices or an increased awareness of the conditions by practitioners.

The most common types of elbow dysplasia are fragmented medial coronoid process (FMCP), ununited anconeal process (UAP), and osteochondrosis of the medial condyle of the humerus. These names refer to assorted abnormalities in the joints and bones that make up the elbow, specifically, the humerus and the ulna.

Symptoms of FMCP, which occurs in young large-breed dogs, may first appear at five to eight months of age. But some Labrador retrievers and rottweilers may not show evidence of the condition for several years. Then the owner may notice that as the dog begins to walk, one limb appears stiff. This lameness may be more apparent when the animal first rises or after extensive exercise. There might also be a thickening or enlargement over the inside area of the elbow. In older dogs the joint may "pop" or "click."

Golden and Labrador retrievers, Bernese mountain dogs, rottweilers, and German shepherds are commonly afflicted with FMCP, as are Australian shepherds, Newfoundlands, Saint Bernards, mastiffs, springer spaniels, chow chows, shar-peis, Shetland sheepdogs, some terriers and setters, and even mixed breeds. As is true for other forms of elbow dysplasia, surgery can ease some of the discomfort. But since the basic cause is malformation of the joint, arthritis will very likely occur. The best form of therapy is a combination of arthroscopic removal of the FMCP and long-term administration of glucosamine and chondroitin sulfate.

In a dog with UAP, the bony process of the ulna fails to unite to the main portion of the bone because of abnormal pressures within the joint. This can lead to free-floating bone fragments in the elbow joint and eventual osteoarthritis. Again, it is a condition that affects primarily large, rapidly growing dogs, and symptoms of lameness in the foreleg(s) are generally first seen when the animals are young. There may be popping and cracking when the elbow is manipulated and increased discomfort when the elbow joint is extended.

UAP may be caused by trauma or injury, genetics, joint abnormalities, or metabolic factors. Many breeds of dog suffer from UAP, including German shepherds, Great Pyrenees, Great Danes, Irish wolfhounds, English mastiffs, Newfoundlands, bloodhounds, pointers, weimaraners, and Saint Bernards. Smaller dogs such as French bulldogs, basset hounds, and dachshunds can also develop the condition, though. The best form of therapy is a combination of surgery to reattach the fragment and long-term administration of glucosamine and chondroitin sulfate.

Canine patella luxation (CPL): This condition affects the knee, or stifle joints, of a wide range of canines and is seen more often in larger breeds. Smaller breeds are more likely to develop the form of this condition known as medial luxation (MPL), as opposed to lateral luxation (LPL). Recently, however, MPL has emerged in larger breeds, such as Akitas, Doberman pinschers, Labrador retrievers, and Newfoundlands. If canine hip dysplasia is present in a large breed, there is a greater chance of also developing CPL. Dogs can be affected at an early age, from ten to twelve months old, but symptoms often don't manifest themselves until the animals are brought to a veterinarian for this problem, when they're two years old or more. For reasons that remain a mystery, female dogs are one and a half times more likely to incur CPL as male dogs.

Signs of CPL: A dog with CPL may "skip" or lock its leg to complete non-weight-bearing activity with the hind legs. This lameness may be on one or both sides. There may be only minimal discomfort when the leg is manipulated. Often, in between episodes of lameness, the dog walks normally. Surgery is often needed to correct this problem.

Poor Nutrition

Recent research reveals that nutrition can influence the inflammatory process that is sometimes involved in arthritis, as well as affect the development of orthopedic diseases such as osteoarthritis. One study has cited overfeeding as one example of poor nutrition. Excess calories leads to rapid growth, a well-known risk factor for hip dysplasia and osteoarthritis, especially in fast-growing, large-breed dogs.[14]

In addition, foods such as red meat contain certain types of fatty acids that promote production of hormone-like substances known as prostaglandins. These compounds not only can trigger inflammation but can make it worse.

Chapter 7 takes a more in-depth look at healthy diets and the ways in which poor nutrition increases the risk of developing osteoarthritis.

Injury

Osteoarthritis and degeneration of cartilage can develop when there is trauma to the cartilage or to the bone located directly under this cartilage. Repeated stress to a joint can have the same effect as trauma. In both cases a cycle of cartilage destruction and bone spur formation results.

In one study on acquired conditions that lead to osteoarthritis in canines, researchers found that once joint cartilage is damaged, the new replacement cartilage is likely to be inferior to the original. As a result, osteoarthritis will very likely occur in this joint at some point. The study authors concluded that pet owners should be aware that timely and careful management of an injured joint can help minimize permanent damage and delay the onset of arthritis symptoms.[15]

Always take your dog to a veterinarian if it is involved in an accident of any kind, even if it seems normal. Traumatic physical events, like being hit by a car or jumping from unusual heights, can damage ligaments and soft tissues as well as fracture joints. Even young dogs that play very hard or engage in any demanding activities should be checked by a veterinarian for joint soundness.

Taking steps now to correct any problems can prevent — or at least delay — the onset of arthritis in the future.

Signs That Your Pet May Have Arthritis

A 1997 article appearing in a professional veterinarians' journal listed various observable signs of developing osteoarthritis in cats that are also typical behaviors in other animals.[16] By observing your own pet's behavior and comparing it with this list, you can determine whether symptoms of osteoarthritis are occurring and take appropriate action.

Movement

Movements that were once smooth and flowing become stiff and awkward. This change is particularly noticeable in cats, which typically have greater flexibility in their movements. You may observe a limited range of motion in one or more joints. Although it could be subtle in the beginning, such a change may become more noticeable in time. Lameness or limping is another clue that there are problems in the joints.

Pain

This is a key symptom of the disease, and one of the most frustrating for pet owners because our animals cannot describe how they feel. Arthritis pain can range from a mild and moderately dull aching to a deep throbbing. In the early stages of the disease, this pain may be only a minor ache that occurs after a joint is used. This sort usually disappears with rest. In later stages of the disease, any movement of the joint can cause a sharp pain. Eventually the joint may also ache at rest and can disrupt sleep. Be on the alert for signs of restlessness.

An animal experiencing pain as it moves a certain joint might hesitate when walking or hold the affected limb in a particular position. It may wince or flinch when the joint is used or when certain places on the body are touched. A pet that once liked to be cuddled or lifted up onto a person's lap may resist being handled, picked up, or cradled in its owner's arms. This may be due to excess fluid accumulating in the tissues surrounding the joint, making the area painful to touch or move. Sometimes you can see swelling in the affected area, but not always. Even if there is no swelling, the joint could still be arthritic.

Ill Temper, Staying in Hiding, Being Nervous, Weakness

If an animal is ill and in pain, it feels vulnerable, especially when it is confronted by another animal or picked up carelessly by its owner. Unable to flee or adjust its position to avoid discomfort, the pet may avoid these situations by hiding or becoming grouchy.

Depression

An animal that is experiencing discomfort or pain may withdraw. A cat or dog that is normally very involved with its owner may become unresponsive and fail to greet people when they arrive home, for example. Or a usually playful animal might refuse to chase a ball or bat a toy mouse. Depression might manifest itself as a sad look in the eyes or a dejected posture.

Appetite

A cat or dog that is normally ready, willing, and able to eat could experience a loss of appetite or make only a passing attempt at eating the foods it usually enjoys. If your pet decides not to eat for a day or two, this may not necessarily indicate osteoarthritis. But it is cause for concern and may require a visit to the veterinarian.

Sleep

A pet that begins to sleep abnormally long hours each day may be suffering from osteoarthritis. Pets with osteoarthritis spend more time sleeping because activity is less pleasant. Cats, which normally sleep and nap intermittently throughout the day and night, might increase their already extensive downtime.

Incontinence and Abnormal Urination Behavior

Arthritic pets may begin to urinate in the house, simply because it is too painful to go outside or use the litter box. Of course, abnormal urination is a symptom of many other diseases, so a veterinarian should be consulted.

Diagnosing Arthritis in Pets

A veterinarian may check for osteoarthritis with manual manipulation — by bending and flexing the joint in the suspected area — looking for the following signs:

- limited range of movement of joints
- pain resulting from manipulation
- audible cracking or grinding of the joint (*crepitus*)
- tenderness to the touch in the suspected area
- lameness and gait abnormalities
- muscle atrophy

X Rays and Other Technological Tools

A veterinarian may decide to confirm a diagnosis with a simple X ray, which can reveal changes in the bone adjacent to the cartilage, a sign of osteoarthritis. One indicator of arthritis is the presence of osteophytes (a bony outgrowth, often called a bone spur), which occur when there is abnormal stress on the joint. There may also be a narrowing of the joint spaces. If the disease is advanced, there may also be extensive loss of cartilage, as well as bone spurs and abnormal density of the subchondral bone.

More sophisticated technology, including computerized tomography (CT scans), arthroscopy (which provides a view of the interior of the joint), and magnetic resonance (MR) imaging, might also be used to complete the diagnosis. In animals and humans alike, arthroscopy is becoming the method of choice for diagnosis and surgical treatment of joint problems.

Various studies have been conducted in recent years to assess whether MR imaging is an adequate tool for assessing osteoarthritis in animals. In a German study published in November 1995, a team of researchers headed by C. C. Nolte-Ernsting concluded that, using an animal osteoarthritis model, MR imaging provided the highest standard in noninvasive diagnosis of the presence of osteophytes in the knee.[17]

The reality is, however, that MR imaging is still very expensive and not always an option for pet owners. With the availability of lower-cost diagnostic alternatives, you may want to consult with your veterinarian about the best tools to determine whether your pet has arthritis.

What Are Not the Signs of Osteoarthritis?

There are many changes that can occur to an animal as it ages, and not all of them are osteoarthritis. The following are not symptoms of arthritis:

- collapsing when walking, knuckling of the feet, or dragging the legs (likely a neurological problem)
- swelling of the limbs not near the joint
- pain in a long bone, such as the foreleg
- a joint that is painful and hot to the touch (usually indicative of infection). Always consult with your veterinarian if your animal displays any unusual symptoms.

Clinical Differences Between Osteoarthritis and Rheumatoid Arthritis

As mentioned earlier, there are significant differences between these two diseases. Rheumatoid arthritis is a disorder of the immune system that affects the body's connective tissues. Symptoms include fatigue, weakness, fever, anemia, and other health problems, including inflamed joints. Unlike osteoarthritis, rheumatoid arthritis usually develops on both sides of the body at once — for instance, either both ankle (hock) or both wrist (carpal) joints.

The severity of joint destruction is much greater with rheumatoid arthritis. While osteoarthritis is more common in the knee, hip, and elbow, rheumatoid arthritis usually affects smaller joints, such as the ankle and the bones between the toes and the wrist (metacarpals). With rheumatoid arthritis, there is also a generalized feeling of fatigue and sickness, accompanied by fever and weight loss.

Rheumatoid arthritis is a fairly rare condition and usually occurs only in small and toy breeds of dogs and in cats.

How Osteoarthritis Affects Other Animals

Osteoarthritis can afflict household pets, but larger animals and various mammals may also develop the disease. There is considerable research documenting its occurrence in horses. The focus is most often on racehorses, simply because their economic value has made it a necessity to understand and treat this disease. Goats, calves, sheep, pigs, deer, reindeer, and guinea pigs are also mentioned in the scientific literature on osteoarthritis.

Damage in horses due to osteoarthritis can be significant, as a study of twenty-five active or retired Thoroughbred race-horses by researchers at the College of Veterinary Medicine, Louisiana State University, Baton Rouge, documents. Those with observable lameness or sensitivity to bending their ankle joints (also known as the fetlock, or *metacarpophalangeal* region) were compared with horses that were clinically normal and not lame.[18]

Joints showing osteoarthritis had significantly elevated pressure within the joint and increased stiffening of the soft tissue as well as a decrease in range of motion. In fact, compared with the other clinical conditions, osteoarthritis resulted in the greatest reduction in flexion. Thoroughbreds assessed with no joint difficulties had a mean range of joint motion of 60.81 degrees in the fetlock, while joint movement in the osteoarthritic horses was measured at half this amount, with only 30.80 degrees of mobility.[19]

Of course, domesticated animals aren't the only ones suffering from osteoarthritis. Any animal with a bony skeleton can develop the disease, including those in the wild as well as in zoos. In some cases these fellow creatures provide valuable insights into treatment programs. At the Los Angeles Zoo, for example, where 20 percent of the twelve hundred animals are senior citizens, arthritis is a fairly common ailment, particularly in large, heavy animals, like elephants and rhinos. Not surprisingly, their symptoms are similar to those we observe in our house pets. When an elderly, forty-some-year-old Asian elephant named Gita has difficulty rising and walking around, her keepers till the hard-packed soil in her enclosure to make it softer, then give her ibuprofen and warm-water soaks to ease the pain in her achy joints. Romulus, an arthritic red-maned wolf, also takes pain relievers and lies under a heat lamp to help keep his joints flexible.[20]

In addition, Romulus and many others are being treated with the same supplements that are at the core of *The Arthritis Cure for Pets,* with outstanding results. Before we look at those supplements in more detail, though, let's examine the role of a group of pain relievers known as nonsteroidal anti-inflammatory drugs (NSAIDs) in treating arthritis in your pet.

What You Should Know About NSAIDs

For those of us who cherish our pets, keeping them free from pain is always a high priority. But since animals can't complain or verbally describe what they're feeling, it can sometimes be difficult to tell what — or even if — they are suffering. As noted earlier, cats' flexibility makes them able to maintain normal movement in spite of joint soreness or difficulty using a limb. And dogs, always eager to accompany their human companions, may show only a slight limp or hesitancy that does not reflect the degree of pain they are actually feeling.

> *Princess, a twelve-year-old shepherd mix, for example, was an extremely active dog, always ready to chase a tennis ball or go for a hike. She showed no signs of lameness, although Rob, her owner, did notice one day that when they were just setting off on a hike, Princess moved her rear legs in a sort of "hop" for the first couple of minutes. After going a quarter mile or so, she would settle into her normal gait, and Rob assumed she was just "getting older."*

It wasn't until Princess went to the veterinarian for her annual vaccinations that it was discovered she did not like her hips or rear legs touched. An X ray confirmed what the doctor suspected — Princess had arthritis in her hip joints. The odd hopping at the beginning of a hike was simply her way of easing the pain until her joints were "warmed up."

As the veterinarian discussed the situation with Rob, it was obvious he felt guilty for letting his beloved dog suffer all these months. Even worse, his father had arthritis so severely that he had sold his plumbing business and retired early because of the pain. Rob was concerned that the veterinarian's diagnosis was the "beginning of the end" for Princess as well. But as his veterinarian assured him, there were many more hikes in Princess's future. With the proper medication, she would be able to cope with the condition and continue to live just as actively as before. "What you have to remember," the veterinarian told Rob, "is that just because she's getting older doesn't mean she has to slow down. Once, that was true, but today we can keep her relatively free of pain and keep her moving. So don't put away the tennis balls or the hiking shoes. Exercise is very important for dogs with arthritis, and with the many options available today, movement won't be a problem."

A Closer Look at Pain

Pain in itself is not an illness. It is a symptom, the body's way of telling us something is wrong. There are essentially two types of pain: acute and chronic. Acute pain is short lived. If your dog strains a muscle, for example, or if your cat gets wounded in a fight with another cat, it feels acute pain. Painkillers are sometimes needed, but the situation corrects itself in six weeks or less.

Chronic pain, on the other hand, lasts for more than six weeks and accompanies such serious ailments as cancer (as well as arthritis). Because animals differ greatly in their ability to tolerate pain, ordinary painkillers may work wonders for one pet and do nothing for another. Even when standard pain therapy does not work, though, there are other options, both pharmaceutical and alternative.

The pain that occurs with arthritis is the body's way of allowing the afflicted joint to rest. With many conditions, avoiding use, and the additional damage it would cause, is a necessity for proper healing. Sports injuries like sprains and strains are often treated with the RICE approach (rest, ice, compress, elevate), in both humans and animals. But with arthritis, rest alone — or even with the other RICE components — is not enough to heal the joint.

In fact, becoming sedentary is one of the worst things an arthritis sufferer can do. Exercise can ease the animal's pain by strengthening the muscles around the afflicted joint, thereby stabilizing and supporting the joint by taking away some of the pressure. (Of course, if exercise leads to weight loss, it lightens the burden even more.) As discussed in greater detail later in the book, exercise also keeps bones strong, increases circulation, delivers essential nutrients to cartilage, increases synovial fluid, and helps prevent joint deformities.

In order to make exercise possible for many arthritis sufferers, painkillers are often recommended. The best course of action is to use painkillers intermittently as needed to reduce pain and inflammation while exercise and supplements are used long term to promote optimal joint health and function. In some cases, though, painkillers may be needed for long-term treatment. Regardless of which category your pet is in, it is good to understand how animals feel pain, as well as how the different types of painkillers work to eliminate it.

Feeling the Pain

All mammals have nerve receptors in their skin, muscles, and joints. The nerve receptors in humans and animals are activated in three different ways. First, they respond to contact, whether a gentle touch or petting or something much more harsh, such as falling or being hit. Second, nerve receptors react to changes in temperature. When a dog or cat gets too hot, for example, it seeks out a shady spot, because its nerve receptors have sent an appropriate signal to the brain. Similarly, if an animal feels too cold, it goes in search of warmth. Third, nerve receptors react to chemicals in the body such as prostaglandins. Stimulated cells relay messages to the brain, where they are converted to the sensation of pain.

In both humans and animals, the body responds to pain by releasing its own painkillers, known as endorphins, which help us continue to function in spite of aches or even more serious pain. Endorphins are natural opiates, the same substances that produce a feeling of well-being after exercise that is sometimes called "runner's high," which is another reason why exercise can benefit arthritis sufferers.

If you suspect that your pet is in pain, the best way to determine a course of treatment is to visit the veterinarian. In addition to the standard physical examination, the veterinarian may run blood and urine tests, take X rays, and possibly perform an ultrasound. These diagnostic tools give a detailed picture of the animal's overall health, as well as an indication of how severe its pain may be. Without this information, it is difficult — not to mention risky — to prescribe painkillers. A cat that has pulled a tendon may need short-term pain relief, for example, while a dog with serious hip dysplasia requires an entirely different medication.

Don't Do It Yourself

Many well-intentioned pet owners short-cut this approach by doing their own diagnoses and giving their pets over-the-counter painkillers that they take themselves. There are a number of reasons you should not do so. First, although some dogs can tolerate certain human medications, cats do not fare as well. Buffered aspirin, for example, is tolerated well by some dogs but can cause severe reactions in cats, as does acetaminophen (Tylenol and related products) and ibuprofen (Motrin, among others). These products can cause everything from nausea and vomiting to convulsions to death. In fact, just one Extra-Strength Tylenol can be fatal to a cat. If you find that your cat has been given — or somehow ingested — these products, try to induce vomiting immediately. Or simply go straight to the veterinarian. This situation should be treated as an emergency.

We should mention that there have been instances of veterinarians' recommending small amounts of aspirin to treat various ailments in cats. The dose and frequency of the treatment should be followed precisely to avoid the possibility of developing toxic side effects.

As for dogs, buffered or enteric-coated aspirin (which is easier on the stomach than the unbuffered variety) is an acceptable pain reliever, although, again, this is an area of controversy among veterinarians. Not all agree that buffered aspirin protects against the upset stomach and possible ulcers that can result from steady aspirin intake. A recent study at Virginia Tech's College of Veterinary Medicine found small ulcers in the stomachs of dogs taking aspirin even though they were not showing clinical signs of discomfort. Still, some veterinarians do feel that aspirin is appropriate and effective, as well as a less costly, alternative to similar products designed specifically for pets.

Do not treat a dog or cat with either acetaminophen or ibuprofen. While both these NSAIDs are popular with humans, they can be toxic to animals. In dogs, these drugs cause severe stomach problems, including ulcers. And, as noted earlier, acetaminophen can be fatal to a cat.

How Much Aspirin Is Enough for My Dog?

Because of the increased safety and effectiveness of new approved NSAIDs for dogs, the practice of giving aspirin to dogs has dramatically decreased. However, if your dog is prescribed aspirin, here are some things to keep in mind.

Aspirin is usually measured either in milligrams (mg) or in grains, and a 5-grain tablet equals 325 mg. If you have a product that is labeled in milligrams, the recommended dosage, which should be given twice a day, is one-fourth of a 325 mg tablet for each ten pounds your dog weighs. So, for example, if Rusty weighs in at sixty pounds, he should be receiving six one-quarter tablets, which is the same as one and a half aspirin. Meanwhile, little Suzy, who only weighs ten pounds, would take only one-quarter of a tablet. If your dog falls in between the ten-pound guidelines — and weighs thirty-six pounds, for example, or twenty-two pounds — ask your veterinarian if you should stay with the lower dosage or round off to the next weight.

If the aspirin you are using is measured in grains, the guidelines are one 5-grain tablet for every sixty pounds of weight, given every twelve hours.

Since even buffered or enteric-coated aspirin can cause stomach problems, especially if taken for long periods of time, watch for any signs of upset stomach — including vomiting, refusal to eat, or diarrhea — in your dog.

Always check with your veterinarian before administering aspirin.

How to Give a Pet Medicine

The professional method, favored by veterinarians and animal-health technicians, looks simple but can be tricky for the average pet owner. The first step is to get the pet's mouth open (not always an easy feat, since animals seem to know when medicine is involved). Find the space behind the canine tooth in the top row of your pet's teeth. Put your thumb in the space and pull the top of the jaw upward, then quickly drop the pill in its mouth, as far back on the tongue as possible. This method may be easier for the novice if there are two people involved. In that case, one lifts the top jaw while pulling down on the lower jaw with the other hand, while the second person inserts the pill.

If this method doesn't work after two or three tries, stop. Stressing your pet — and yourself — does no one any good and may even result in problem behavior. Instead of forcing the issue, go to Plan B. This tried-and-true option solves the pilling problem for most animals, although cats are still somewhat tricky. Basically a two-step process, it involves getting a morsel of favorite food — cheese, bread, meat, fish, or whatever your pet prefers — and hiding the pill inside it. Or try coating the pill with something such as peanut butter or cream cheese. The trick is to hide the pill in an amount of food that is likely to be gulped down quickly, rather than being chewed and swallowed. Now simply offer it to your pet and let nature take its course. Dogs generally swallow the treat — and pill — immediately, although they might work the food loose from particularly strong-smelling medicines and spit them out. Keep a lookout for pills that land on the floor, and try again.

Cats aren't quite as easy to pill this way, since they don't gulp their food as dogs do. If hiding the pill in food doesn't do the trick, try coating the pill with a little butter or cream cheese, then go back to the professional method. The additions of tasty flavor and a texture that goes down smoothly often help.

All About Analgesics

Drugs that relieve pain are known as analgesics, an umbrella term that includes everything from aspirin to opium. From the pet point of view, the most important analgesics are in the category known as nonsteroidal anti-inflammatory drugs (NSAIDs). These are fast-acting medications that can quickly remedy a pet's discomfort. Such medications allow an animal to continue its daily activities, like feeding, exercising, and sleeping, without pain. It is estimated that there are as many as 30 million people and 8 million dogs consuming NSAIDs worldwide.

NSAIDs Are Not a Cure

Let's make one thing perfectly clear: painkillers are an adjunct to other, more long-term therapies designed to restore cartilage and repair joints. During the weeks and months it may take for healing to occur, NSAIDs play a *supporting* role in the process. In other words, although they can be highly effective at reducing symptoms such as swelling, inflammation, and pain, they are not cures for osteoarthritis. NSAIDs can make living with osteoarthritis more tolerable for

> NSAIDs play an important role in controlling pain and inflammation associated with osteoarthritis in dogs. Rimadyl is an effective new drug and is the most common NSAID used in dogs in the United States.

an animal, but they do not treat the disease itself. Supplements such as glucosamine and chondroitin sulfate, which have the ability to work at the cellular level to restore damaged cartilage and help it heal, are aimed at treating the disease itself.

Painkillers and Pets

Any treatment plan for osteoarthritis needs to be tailored to the individual case. In selecting a medication, it is important to consider the animal's age, size, and sensitivity to drugs, if such information is available.

It is also important to be consistent in giving any medication to your pet. In some cases, it may take several weeks or even months before you see positive results. If you are tempted to stop a medication, first inform your veterinarian. It can be a shock to the animal's system to stop some drugs abruptly.

> Do not administer any medication to your pet, whether prescription or over-the-counter, without consulting with your veterinarian first. Some medications can be dangerous for certain animals, and using human-weight-dosage guidelines can be dangerous, as dosage amounts vary dramatically between humans and animals.

The following are medications that many people commonly use to diminish joint pain. Your veterinarian may prescribe one or more of them for your pet. Some are available by prescription only. Others are sold over the counter and are commonly found in most households.

Nonsteroidal Anti-Inflammatory Drugs (NSAIDs)

This class of medications is taken to reduce inflammation, swelling, and pain. Human and animal patients with arthritis take them to reduce joint inflammation, thereby permitting an improved quality of life with more freedom of movement. There are more than one hundred different NSAID medications available for sale or being researched. Nonprescription NSAIDs include such familiar medications as Advil, Aleve, Nuprin, Excedrin-IB, Midol 200, aspirin, Motrin, and Orudis. This class of medications is the most commonly recommended by veterinarians for the treatment of musculoskeletal and arthritic conditions.[21] These drugs can make it possible to reduce and terminate other medications that have more severe side effects, such as corticosteroids. It is estimated that between 70 million and 75 million prescriptions for NSAIDs are written each year, representing approximately $2 billion in sales. There are six major classes of NSAIDs (see "An NSAID Primer"). The best known is the group called salicylic acids, which includes aspirin.

The recommended prescription NSAIDs for dogs include Carprofen (sold as Rimadyl) and Etodolac (sold as Etogesic). These drugs must be obtained through a veterinarian. Good results have been obtained using these NSAIDs to treat certain types of pets with arthritis. A study examining the use of anti-inflammatories for pain reduction and inflammation associated with arthritis showed that dogs in particular can get good results when the dosage is administered properly and consistently over time.[22]

Cats are usually treated with a combination approach that may include an NSAID product in conjunction with complementary therapies and supplements.[23] *It cannot be overemphasized that NSAIDs must be used very carefully in cats, and only under a veterinarian's close supervision.*

How NSAIDs Function to Lessen and Eliminate Pain

NSAIDs prevent pain by blocking production of prostaglandins. These hormonelike compounds — named after the prostate gland, where they were first isolated in 1930 — are actually found throughout the body. They are responsible for regulating many functions of the cells in all tissues. Although these versatile substances are still being studied, we already know a great deal about them.

For example, we know that prostaglandins have a wide range of functions. Some control activity in the involuntary or smooth muscles in blood vessels. Others lower blood flow, protect the gastrointestinal system, or reduce blood stickiness. There are also other prostaglandins that produce the opposite effect. In a state of health, prostaglandins are produced in a balanced ratio so that the opposing actions are in harmony. The balance between the various types of prostaglandins affects cardiovascular and gastrointestinal health, as well as other activities in the body.

When a pet develops osteoarthritis and cells are damaged, an enzyme known as cyclooxygenase (COX) initiates production of a specific type of prostaglandin that triggers inflammation. Taking an NSAID blocks the production of this "bad" prostaglandin but also interferes with the production of other "good" prostaglandins, disrupting the overall balance of these substances. The resulting imbalance can cause serious side effects, such as vomiting, bleeding, or kidney failure.

All six major classes of NSAIDs share the ability to inhibit the COX enzyme. But it was the recent discovery of two forms of COX — aptly named COX-1 and COX-2 — that has made it possible to refine NSAIDs in such a way that many of the negative side effects can be eliminated. That is because of the two forms of cyclooxygenase, only COX-2 is predominately involved in the inflammatory response, while COX-1 actually protects tissues in the kidneys and digestive tract.

Since this discovery, scientists have developed drugs known as COX-2 inhibitors, such as Rimadyl and Etogesic, which preferentially stop the "bad" prostaglandins and leave the "good" ones untouched. The COX-2 inhibitors have the anti-inflammatory power of aspirin with fewer side effects.[24]

A Drug's Effectiveness Depends on Its Half-Life

Half-life is the amount of time a drug remains in the system at a level high enough to be therapeutic. NSAIDs generally have either a short half-life (less than six hours) or a long half-life (more than ten hours). Both forms have drawbacks, which need to be considered when selecting a medication for your pet.

Short-acting NSAIDs: These are quickly absorbed into the system and produce fast results, but they are also quickly excreted. As a result, short-acting NSAIDs are less likely to accumulate in the body at toxic levels and there is less risk of side effects. These medications need to be administered more frequently, however, which can be a nuisance, especially with animals that resist taking their medicine.

Long-acting NSAIDs: With these medications, one daily dose may be all that is necessary. These drugs are stronger, however, and remain in the body for longer periods of time, posing a greater risk of toxic accumulation and side effects. They are not recommended if other serious health conditions also exist, such as kidney problems.

General Guidelines for Taking NSAIDs

These medications should be given at mealtime. It is a good idea to allow the animal to begin eating, then take the medication, and finish eating. With this method, the drug is absorbed along with the food and the gastrointestinal tract is optimally protected. Some veterinarians also prescribe an additional medication to help prevent ulcers, a possible side effect with long-term use of these drugs.

> **CAUTION!**
>
> If you forget to give your pet its medication, *don't* then double the dosage the next round. NSAIDs should not be given to an animal that is pregnant. And if your pet is having surgery, inform your veterinarian that your pet is taking NSAIDs. These drugs can inhibit platelets, which play an important role in blood clotting.

Side Effects of NSAIDs

In general, these medications are well tolerated by most pets. Careful monitoring is still recommended, though, because they do have more potentially dangerous side effects. For example, a two- to threefold increase in gastrointestinal bleeding in patients using NSAIDs has been reported. Observable symptoms may include vomiting, diarrhea, constipation, nausea, and cramps. NSAIDs can also damage the liver or kidneys, which may aggravate preexisting hypertension.

Guidelines for Reducing the Side Effects of NSAIDs

- Always give medication with food or with an antacid, if your veterinarian recommends it.
- Do not combine them with food that may irritate the intestinal tract, such as table scraps for a dog unaccustomed to eating human food.
- Be sure to call the veterinarian if signs of toxicity develop, such as vomiting, loss of appetite, dark stools, jaundice, or lethargy.

How NSAIDs Can Actually Worsen Arthritis

In addition to the side effects already discussed, there is another, potentially serious concern related to NSAIDs. Based on animal experiments, there is evidence that NSAIDs can actually damage cartilage, which, of course, makes existing osteoarthritis worse.

This can happen in two ways. Some NSAIDs slow cartilage repair and increase cartilage destruction. In addition, just by minimizing the pain in a damaged joint, they can encourage excess activity and further damage the cartilage.

To avoid these problems, the use of NSAIDs should be limited. And the best way to do that is to combine NSAIDs with glucosamine and chondroitin sulfate, decreasing the amount of painkillers as discomfort and limping disappear and cartilage is repaired. This approach makes doubly good sense because the effectiveness of these painkillers may plateau after a time, allowing the discomfort to return. Chapter 5 presents the total regimen — the Six-Step Arthritis Cure for Pets Program — the step-by-step approach to getting your pet healthy and happy again.

> Caprofen (Rimadyl), a new NSAID for dogs, has been found in recent research to have a reduced tendency for cartilage destruction, compared with other drugs such as aspirin.

An NSAID Primer

Your veterinarian has many types of anti-inflammatory drugs to choose from.

Salicylic Acids

The active ingredient in all drugs of this class is salicylic acid. The most well-known name in this group of medications is aspirin; others include Disalcid, Dolobid, Mono-Gesic, and Salflex. The use of aspirin predates modern medicine by a hundred and fifty years, going back to 1758, when the Reverend Edward Stone discovered that an extract from willow tree bark could reduce pain and fever. If your pet is suffering from mild to moderate arthritic pain, aspirin is a possible choice.

Aspirin is not addictive, and its effectiveness does not diminish over time. In low dosages it relieves pain, and at higher dosages it acts as an anti-inflammatory. Be aware that in the case of arthritis, though, joint inflammation responds slowly to aspirin. Neither humans nor animals should take aspirin with other NSAIDs without professional medical supervision.

Side Effects of Aspirin The foremost downside of aspirin for dogs is that it can irritate the stomach and aggravate gastrointestinal problems, such as peptic ulcers. It also stresses the kidneys. Coated or buffered aspirin helps offset these effects. If intestinal bleeding occurs, a dog could develop anemia. Your veterinarian can diagnose anemia with a blood test; either vitamins or foods rich in iron can be added to the dog's diet, such as various organ meats (kidney, heart, and liver) and red meat of all kinds. These are particularly good sources, since the form of iron in animal foods is readily absorbed. *Cats should not be given aspirin unless absolutely necessary and only as prescribed by your veterinarian — it can be fatal if taken at the dog dosage.*

As mentioned earlier, aspirin should always be given with food to avoid upsetting the stomach. Two good forms of aspirin that were developed specifically to solve this problem are buffered and enteric-coated. Buffered aspirin is combined with an antacid to neutralize gastric acid in the stomach, lessening the chance of ulceration. Meanwhile, the enteric-coated variety passes through the stomach before dissolving and is absorbed later, as it moves through the small intestine.

Some doctors believe that enteric-coated aspirin is not absorbed as well, but this is still a matter of debate. It is known, however, that enteric-coated aspirin takes longer to reach the bloodstream and be delivered to tissues where it can dampen pain. As a result, it is not recommended for quick relief.

Proprionic Acid

Various medications fall into this class: Rimadyl, Aleve, Naproxen, Orudis, and Motrin (ibuprofen). In people, ibuprofen is considered a safe and effective treatment for arthritis; *however, toxic side effects have been reported in dogs and cats.* Rimadyl is the medicine of choice for dogs and cats in this class of NSAIDs.

Oxicams

For long-term care, the oxicam medication Feldene (Piroxicam) is often used to reduce inflammation. Feldene is not recommended for dogs, however, because of its long-acting nature and an increased chance of causing gastrointestinal ulceration and perforation.

Naphthylalkanones

Drugs in this class, including Relafen, are recommended for humans with mild to moderate pain. But in dogs they increase the risk of developing ulcers.

Arylacetic Acids

Cataflam and Toradol fall into this class of potent drugs. They cause severe side effects in dogs typical of NSAIDs, including gastrointestinal and kidney disturbances.

Pyranocarboxylic Acids

Lodine is a primary member of this class of medications, which come in a variety of strengths that can be tailored to the patient's needs. Etogesic is approved for use in dogs only.

Other Treatments for Arthritis

Hyaluronic Acid

Several new treatments for arthritis are making their debut. One is hyaluronic acid, a necessary element for the formation of proteoglycans, which, as mentioned earlier, are found in the matrix of cartilage. A typical regimen for hyaluronic acid is an injection once a week for three to five weeks. This dosage can stop pain for several months at a time. Hyaluronic acid has received FDA approval, limited to treating osteoarthritis in the knee.

DMSO

Veterinarians use dimethyl sulfoxide (DMSO), an industrial solvent, as a treatment for musculoskeletal problems in horses (applying it directly to painful joints) and for some skin diseases in dogs.

Side effects of DMSO include a taste of garlic in the mouth, an objectionable and strong odor, skin rashes, headache, nausea, and diarrhea.

As a pain reliever, it has benefits that are comparable to aspirin's.

Muscle Relaxants

Although not used often, except in the case of osteoarthritis in the spine, these medications can be combined with other treatments to control arthritic pain. Valium (diazepam) and metho-carbomol are examples of such drugs. In cases of osteoarthritis, spasms may occur in the muscle surrounding an inflamed joint, triggering pain in the joint as well as in the muscle. Using a muscle relaxant medication can increase flexibility and make it easier for an animal to move normally.

Cortisone and Other Potent Anti-Pain Medications

At one time corticosteroids, including cortisone and prednisone, were the treatments of choice for stopping pain. They are power-ful drugs that provide dramatic and rapid relief. But health experts have discovered that these medications potentially create very serious side effects that can affect osteoarthritis.

Steroids, as they are popularly known, affect the skeletal sys-tem, thinning bones and increasing the risk of fracture. They can trigger demineralization, so that calcium and other essential min-erals are leeched from the bones. Other side effects include weak-ening the immune system and impairing wound healing. If taken over a long period of time, steroids can also lead to diabetes, osteoporosis, hypertension, liver damage, kidney damage, and mental disorders.

Today when corticosteroids are prescribed, they are usually given in far lower doses and for a much shorter duration than in the past. This keeps side effects minimal and makes them an acceptable treatment in some instances.

Steroids are available as pills, eye drops, or creams. They are also sometimes given by injection, locally or deep inside the joint. When a drug of this type is injected directly into the joint, far less of it enters the body than when taken as a pill. Even so, injections should not be given more often than once every three months. Ideally, the time between injections should be between four and six months — longer, if possible.

At first steroids bring relief quickly. But if taken over time, their effectiveness wanes. The body begins to tolerate the drug, and in order to achieve the same effect, the dosage must be increased. Interestingly, the risks involved with taking cortisone injections inspired researchers to develop an alternative. The nonsteroidal anti-inflammatory drugs, many of which were developed in the 1960s, are the result of those efforts. Today cortisone injections are given cautiously, primarily in cases of severe pain. An animal that is receiving cortisone injections should not take NSAIDs at the same time.

> **When several joints are involved in an arthritic condition, steroids are ususally given systemically — in other words, orally rather than by injection. If steroids are taken orally, it is important to taper off this medicine rather than stop it abruptly. Sudden withdrawal can affect hormone production and can lead to serious side effects.**

How to Use Analgesics and NSAIDs in Conjunction with Glucosamine and Chondroitin

Chondroitin sulfate and glucosamine can be combined with a painkiller or nonsteroidal anti-inflammatory drug, especially if an animal shows signs of significant pain. This approach allows the chondroitin sulfate and glucosamine, the core of the famous arthritis cure, to target the actual causes of osteoarthritis. Meanwhile, the painkiller or NSAID reduces the symptoms of the disease. In other words, analgesics and anti-inflammatory drugs alleviate discomfort, but chondroitin sulfate and glucosamine are the key to long-term management of osteoarthritis.

The Arthritis Cure
for Pets

When *The Arthritis Cure* was published in 1997, it created a sensation. At last, millions of arthritis sufferers felt that there was hope they could be helped by something that was harmless, affordable, and — best of all — effective. Not only were there four decades of medical research from around the world supporting glucosamine and chondroitin sulfate — the supplements advocated in the book — but in Europe the same treatment had been used for years with great success. Because of a complicated combination of medical conservatism, commercial obstacles, and consumer attitudes, however, few people in this country were aware that these supplements even existed, let alone that they could relieve suffering.

Unfortunately, physicians weren't the only ones who were slow to embrace this new treatment. American veterinarians, too, resisted the decades' worth of supporting international research and stayed with standard protocols. Finally, however, this research, along with the experiences of a number of leading veterinarians, is creating significant changes in the way osteoarthritis is understood and treated in America.

What we now call the Arthritis Cure is widely known in the United States today, and glucosamine and chondroitin sulfate are two of the most popular nutritional supplements on the market. The preferred form is glucosamine hydrochloride and purified chondroitin sulfates. Let's take a look at a few of the reasons why this rather startling change has occurred.

Dana had never really thought of herself as a dog person until she was given Togo, a young black German shepherd, by her neighbor Carmen, who bred and showed her shepherds all around the country. With his impressive family background, including a number of championship ancestors, Togo seemed to hold great promise. But an early diagnosis of hip dysplasia had cut short her plans to show or breed him. Carmen reasoned that there was no point investing a great deal of time in a dog with congenital health problems: he could not be bred and would probably have to be put down sooner rather than later.

But Dana's heart went out to the young dog, who sat forlornly in his kennel all day while the other dogs were being put through their paces. She offered to take Togo off Carmen's hands, and her neighbor agreed. "But," she warned Dana, "don't get too attached to him. Hip dysplasia is not curable. It's only a matter of time before he won't be able to walk without hip replacement surgery or . . ." She didn't have to finish the sentence; Dana and Carmen both knew what Togo's other option was, and neither wanted to think about it.

As Dana walked Togo down the street to her house, she couldn't help but see how happy he was to be out of the ken-

nel, exploring the real world. But even though they only walked a few hundred feet, Dana couldn't avoid noticing Togo's limp, either. Still, he was a joy to be with — content to sit at her feet while she worked on her paintings, easy to train, calm and yet protective when strangers came around. Her children adored him, and he treated them gently and loved the attention they showered on him. Even Dana's husband, Steve, who had been very skeptical about having a dog in the house, seemed to enjoy his company.

By the end of their first week together, Dana had made a decision. She took Togo to the veterinarian Carmen had recommended and talked to him about hip-replacement surgery. He discussed the expense with her first, but Dana assured him that money was not her first concern. She would take a job teaching art at the local university for a semester or two, or offer private lessons in her home, to earn the extra money. The real issue was Togo. In the one week he'd shared their home, her whole family had fallen in love with the dog. But the limp concerned them. He was only eighteen months old. They simply would not stand by and watch him suffer for the next few years, until the situation became desperate. Something had to be done soon.

The veterinarian described hip-replacement surgery — the risks, the recovery period, and the likely outcome. Dana, who had surgery herself two years before, hated the thought of her poor dog suffering through the healing process. But she also hated the idea of his limping every time he walked. She scheduled a date for the operation and took Togo home.

The following day he went with her on the trip to the local newspaper office, where she placed an ad offering private lessons for aspiring artists in her studio. The woman at the front desk commented on how handsome and well behaved Togo was. "Thank you," she told the clerk. "He's the reason I'm teaching these classes. He's not even two years old yet and he needs hip-replacement surgery. Since there's no Medicare for dogs, I'll be teaching for a while."

"Have you tried the pills they have on the market now?" the clerk asked. "I started my dog on them three months ago, when she started having trouble getting up in the morning. She's fine now — and she's eleven."

When Dana left the newspaper office half an hour later, she was still dubious. But the clerk and two other staffers had spent the past thirty minutes petting Togo and describing how two supplements she'd never heard of — glucosamine and chondroitin sulfate — had cured either their dogs' arthritis or their own! As she watched Togo struggle to climb into the backseat of the car, she knew she should at least try them.

But when she called her veterinarian to ask about the supplements, he told Dana that he thought Togo's problems were so severe that surgery was the only viable option. And he said that he wasn't up on the recent research on glucosamine and chondroitin, so didn't feel comfortable recommending them. However, one of the other professionals he worked with was, and he was happy to refer Dana.

She called the other veterinarian, and two days later Togo was taking a glucosamine–chondroitin sulfate supplement blend, along with a mild pain reliever.

Three weeks later they were able to cancel the appointment for surgery. Togo still limped, but he had definitely *improved. As the new veterinarian had suggested, she and Togo went for short walks to strengthen his muscles. By the end of two months he was like a new dog — jogging several miles three or four days a week, bounding in and out of the car, even jumping on the couch, which Dana let him get away with, since she was so happy he could do it. As for the art lessons, it turned out that most of the students were pet lovers too. The class became a great place to get the latest information on the care and feeding of four-legged companions, and Dana made sure everyone knew about the amazing nutritional supplements that had given Togo what she called "a new leash on life."*

Glucosamine, Chondroitin, and Cartilage

To truly understand how glucosamine and chondroitin sulfate work to improve your pet's health, it is important to know the basic components of cartilage as well as its structure. The word *cartilage* comes from the Latin word *cartilagin,* which means "wickerwork," or "an interlaced series of willows, twigs, or rods." In some ways, this is a very apt description, as we will see later when we discuss the cartilage matrix.

Cartilage is integral to the adult skeleton. It covers the joint surfaces of bone but is not limited to the joints of the limbs. It is also found at certain junctures in the ribs, the nasal septum that divides our nostrils, the outside of our ears, the lining of the Eustachian tubes in the middle ear, the wall of the larynx (where our vocal cords are located), in our respiratory system, and between vertebrae. Interestingly, cartilage also forms the major portion of the embryonic skeleton, providing a model in which most bones develop.

Actually, there are many types of cartilage in the body. When we refer to "cartilage" in the context of osteoarthritis, we are talking about hyaline cartilage, which lines the surfaces of the joints. Hyaline cartilage is also known as joint or "articular" cartilage. Joint cartilage is a smooth, bluish white, opaque, with no nerves or blood supply of its own. When eating chicken or lamb shank, you have come across the rubbery, gelatinous covering at the end of the joint. This is joint cartilage.

As noted earlier, joint cartilage reduces the friction that would be caused by one bone rubbing against another and lessens the stress and strain of the ongoing traumas that we inflict on our joints as we go about our day. While cartilage caps the ends of the bones and absorbs shock, it also provides a slick surface that allows the bone ends to glide easily across each other during movement. There is no material made by man that compares with the shock-absorbing properties and low friction of healthy cartilage.

The Elements of Healthy Cartilage

Healthy cartilage is a dense connective tissue made up of four components: cells, known as "chondrocytes"; collagen; proteoglycans; and water, all of which work together to guarantee smooth, pain-free movement.

Chondrocytes: These special cells are responsible for making new collagen and proteoglycans (see below). The chondrocytes are embedded in a matrix, sometimes called "ground substance." This matrix is compact and firm, giving cartilage the unique structure that allows it to withstand significant tension and pressure. Chondrocytes are found in the matrix's cavities, or *lacunae*, either singly or clustered in groups of two, three, or four.

Chondrocytes play a role in producing new, healthy matrix, as well as removing damaged, unhealthy matrix. The chondrocytes produce enzymes that break down older collagen and proteoglycan molecules so they can be eliminated from the joint when they are no longer functioning properly.

Collagen: Many people are familiar with collagen, because it helps maintain the skin's firmness and promotes a youthful appearance. As a result, it is often added to face creams. But collagen is far more than an ingredient in beauty products. This protein is found in everything from tendons to the cornea within the eye. In cartilage countless tough, ropy collagen "threads" are laid down in crisscross patterns, four layers thick, giving cartilage its elasticity and ability to absorb shock.

Proteoglycans: These huge molecules are composed of protein and sugars. They weave around and through the framework of collagen fibers, forming a dense netting within the cartilage. Conversely, the collagen keeps the proteoglycans in place. Together with water, the proteoglycans and collagen form the cartilage matrix. Like collagen, proteoglycans help keep cartilage resilient. The proteoglycans also trap water and impart the spongelike quality to cartilage. The proteoglycans can attract and hold many times their weight in water.

Water: The main ingredient in healthy cartilage is water. In fact, as much as 65 to 80 percent of cartilage is water.

Giving Nature a Helping Hand: The Role of Glucosamine and Chondroitin Sulfates

Now that you have an idea of the basics of healthy cartilage, you can see why glucosamine and chondroitin sulfate can help pets with osteoarthritis and damaged cartilage.

Glucosamine ensures the creation of healthy cartilage in several ways:

- It is a prime raw material for two substances produced by chondrocytes: the water-attracting proteoglycans and glycosaminoglycans (GAGs), proteins that bind water in the cartilage matrix.
- Glucosamine and chondroitin sulfate are actually more than mere building blocks; they also stimulate the chondrocytes to produce both proteoglycans and GAGs. Research has shown that the amount of proteoglycans produced is directly dependent upon the levels of these substances in the tissues.
- By helping to normalize cartilage metabolism, glucosamine also promotes joint health by slowing the breakdown of cartilage.
- Glucosamine protects existing cartilage and the cartilage growth that it stimulates. The body's natural repair mechanisms are enhanced by glucosamine, which, in turn, assists the body in restoring eroded and damaged cartilage.

At the present time there are no veterinary studies to suggest that isolated use of glucosamine is effective; however, its use in combination with chondroitin sulfate and manganese ascorbate has been found to be synergistic in stimulating cartilage metabolism and inhibiting degradation.[25]

Chondroitin sulfate supplies nutrients to cartilage and inhibits cartilage-degenerating enzymes. It is thought to

- provide substrate (the foundation) for production of new proteoglycans and

• inhibit destructive enzymes that lead to the breakdown of collagen and proteoglycans.

And each molecule of chondroitin sulfate has special chemical properties that give it the ability to attract and hold water in cartilage tissue. If you could peer through an electron microscope, you would see that a proteoglycan molecule has a long backbone, like the trunk of a tree. Extending from this trunk are large branches composed of "core proteins"; extending from each of the branches are as many as one hundred smaller branches. Each small branch is a chain of chondroitin sulfate. In cartilage, a proteoglycan molecule may have as many as ten thousand chains of chondroitin sulfate attached to it.

These chains carry negative electric charges. Consequently, they repel each other, like magnets, which have a positive charge on one side and a negative charge on the other. Place a negatively charged side of one magnet against the positively charged side of another magnet and they attract. Trying to join the two negative — or two positive — sides is futile; they only repel each other.

Similarly, the chondroitin chains have negative electrical charges, which allow them to repel each other. The space that results when the chondroitins separate is the actual matrix of the cartilage, the storage facility for the all-important water supply. Considering the enormous numbers of chondroitin sulfate chains for each proteoglycan molecule, it is easy to see why they are so effective at maintaining high levels of water. The outcome of this action is twofold:

• When water is drawn to these spaces, the cartilage is a spongy, shock-absorbing mass.

- The fluids carry nutrients. This is especially important since, lacking its own blood supply, cartilage has no other way to be nourished.

Enter Osteoarthritis

Given what we now know, let's take another look at osteoarthritis, defined as a disruption of normal cartilage structure and function. We know that several things can occur to interfere with the smooth working of the cartilage. There may be injury, causing partial destruction of cartilage. The trauma may be severe and sudden, as in the case of an animal that has been hit by a car. Or the injury may develop slowly over time, the accumulation of hundreds, if not thousands or more, subtle injuries. An animal that performs under strenuous circumstances, such as a racing greyhound or a show horse that repeatedly jumps fences, may develop osteoarthritis due to repetitive trauma.

Cartilage can deteriorate if an animal is overweight and the obesity places unrelenting pressure on a joint and its cartilage. Cartilage may also break down because of genetics, in which case an animal inherits a tendency for cartilage to age more rapidly than normal.

What Deterioration Looks Like on the Cellular Level

When cartilage is damaged or begins to break down, the cartilage matrix, or "netting," begins to lose its shape and stretch out. At the same time, the proteoglycans lose their grip in the matrix and float away. Once these water-attracting molecules are no longer in place, the cartilage loses its ability to absorb shock. It may then crack, fissure, and eventually wear through completely.

Without the protective cushioning of the cartilage, the bones begin to rub together and can cause an animal severe pain. Small fractures can also develop in the cartilage. The body, which has many natural healing mechanisms, goes into overdrive, producing more bone, cartilage, and synovial fluid.

The new cartilage, however, is usually of inferior quality and fails to cushion the bone ends. With no protection from normal, everyday activities, the bone ends lose their ability to "bend" and absorb shock. In addition, the body may produce more bone to compensate for the deterioration, sometimes leading to bumpy surfaces on the bone ends.

Complicating this condition, the joint lining, or synovium, can become inflamed. There are many nerve endings and pain receptors in the synovium, so the brain receives a message that pain is occurring. In response, the synovium produces extra synovial fluid to lubricate and nourish the joint and smooth the joint action. Although this can be beneficial, the excess fluid production can also cause pain as it stretches the nerve-filled joint capsule.

> As a pet owner, you may be aware only that your animal is limping, but this is what's happening inside the joints: when cartilage is damaged, its surface may become ragged and pockmarks can be seen. These points of stress can eventually wear through completely, creating gaps in the cartilage like those found in a piece of Swiss cheese.

•   •   •

As may be seen from the extensive research done on osteoarthritis in large and small animals, as well as in humans, other remedies may treat the symptoms of the disease, but only glucosamine and chondroitin sulfate can actually repair the damage and prevent more from occurring.

The Scientific Evidence

Until recently research studies looked at the effects of glucosamine and chondroitin sulfate separately because very few products actually combined the two supplements. However, with the success and visibility of *The Arthritis Cure,* scientists and researchers began to develop and test combination products. In the United States the brands Cosamin DS (for humans) and Cosequin (for animals) have been used in most of the research. We recommend these brands as well as PetJoint; however, as other brands are tested and show clinical efficacy, our list of recommended products will surely grow. Combination products have been used in two important American human studies.

Science Teams Glucosamine and Chondroitin

In the first randomized, placebo-controlled clinical study in the United States, ninety-three patients from the Hendersonville Orthopedic Clinic in Hendersonville, North Carolina, were given Cosamin DS, which contains 500 mg of glucosamine hydrochloride, 400 mg of sodium chondroitin sulfate, and 76 mg of manganese ascorbate, daily for six months. Seventy-one of the participants had mild to moderate osteoarthritis of the knee, and twenty-one suffered from severe osteoarthritis of the knee.

> Manganese ascorbate has been shown to be an essential element for proteoglycan synthesis. Most commercial dog foods contain adequate amounts of manganese. However, pets that are fed homemade diets may be lacking this mineral, so be sure that the product you purchase contains manganese.

Results showed that 52 percent of the intervention group responded to treatment. And researchers concluded that "glucosamine and chondroitin sulfate are effective for the treatment of pain and the loss of function associated with OA [osteoarthritis] of the knee. More importantly, these agents have no known side effects."[26] In medical research, double-blind, placebo-controlled studies are considered the most valuable. They involve two groups of participants with similar symptoms. One group is given the medication or supplement that is being tested, while the other receives a "sugar pill," also known as a placebo. Because neither the researchers nor the participants know who is getting the real medication and who is receiving the placebo, these studies are considered to be objective and less likely to be influenced by expectations.

•   •   •

The elite Naval Amphibious Forces, otherwise known as the Navy Seals, have a high incidence of osteoarthritis of the knees and back. Thirty-four Seals with osteoarthritis of the knee or lower back were given the following dosage of Cosamin DS — 1,500 mg of glucosamine, 1,200 mg of chondroitin sulfate, and 228 mg of manganese ascorbate — daily for sixteen weeks.

Researchers concluded that the combination therapy was found to be effective to relieve the symptoms of osteoarthritis of the knee. However, there were no conclusive findings for osteoarthritis of the back.[27]

A Separate Look at Glucosamine and Chondroitin Sulfate

In addition to these groundbreaking studies on the combination of the two supplements, there is a significant body of scientific research on the effectiveness of the supplements as separate agents.

Science Puts Glucosamine to the Test

In Europe more than twelve hundred arthritis sufferers were given 1.5 grams of glucosamine in three daily doses for an average of fifty days. The results were impressive. Not only did pain steadily improve during the treatment period, but a whopping 95 percent of the patients reported "sufficient" or "good" results. There were no side effects in 86 percent of the participants, meaning glucosamine was tolerated by far more patients than any pharmaceutical. And after the subjects stopped taking the supplements, glucosamine continued to work for up to three months.[28]

Several double-blind studies have compared glucosamine with over-the-counter pain relievers such as ibuprofen.

In one eight-week-long trial, forty patients suffering from arthritis of the knee were given either 1.2 grams of ibuprofen daily or 1.5 grams of glucosamine sulfate. (There are four forms of nonprescription glucosamine available, and all are salts of glucosamine. Glucosamine sulfate is the one that is generally used in European research, but the others — hydrochloride and hydroiodide — should work just as well. A person or pet with thyroid problems should not take the hydroiodide form, though. N-acetyl has been shown not to be effective, and hydrochloride has more bioactive glucosamine than the sulfate form.)

Although initially those taking ibuprofen experienced faster pain relief than the patients taking glucosamine, this effect tapered off after two weeks. Meanwhile, the glucosamine group had sustained pain relief during the study. In addition, when they were asked to score their pain at the end of the trial, those who took glucosamine rated their pain at only 0.8 (on a scale from zero to three, with three being the most painful). But the ibuprofen group ranked their pain at 2.2.[29]

A similar study also determined that glucosamine sulfate was just as effective at pain relief as ibuprofen but had fewer adverse reactions. Of the 100 patients receiving ibuprofen in the study, thirty-five complained of side effects, while only six of those taking glucosamine reported negative effects.[30]

Glucosamine's ability to generate healthy new cartilage was amply demonstrated in a month-long Italian study involving eighty patients with severe osteoarthritis. The participants who received glucosamine showed significant improvement in overall symptoms, with a full 20 percent becoming completely free of symptoms. But more significantly, when researchers examined cartilage samples from the patients who had been taking glucosamine, they discovered that the samples resembled healthy cartilage, while the samples taken from the placebo group were clearly damaged.[31]

Chondroitin's Clinical Success

In France, for example, chondroitin sulfate's pain-relieving abilities were compared with a placebo in a double-blind, randomized study of 120 people suffering from osteoarthritis of the knee and hip. One group received oral chondroitin sulfate, while the other was given a placebo. Both groups also took the same doses of NSAIDs. After ninety days the patients who took chondroitin sulfate experienced "significant improvement in pain and pain function." In addition, no side effects were noted. But there was one unexpected benefit. Post-research follow-up determined that the improvements in the chondroitin sulfate group lasted for two full months after the study had concluded and participants were no longer taking the supplements![32]

In another study from France, researchers found that damaged cartilage had been repaired in a group of patients who had been given chondroitin sulfate for ninety days, while no repair had occurred in the control group, who had received standard pain medication.[33]

These are only a sampling of the studies that have been conducted worldwide. The bottom line is that both glucosamine and chondroitin sulfate are effective, safe treatments for osteoarthritis in people.

The Arthritis Cure Works for People and for Pets

While useful to know that these supplements help ease the suffering of humans with osteoarthritis, as explained in Chapter 3, drugs intended for humans are not always suitable for animals. So you may be wondering about the effects of glucosamine and chondroitin on your pet. First, keep in mind that these supplements are "nutraceuticals," compounds of naturally occurring substances, not pharmaceuticals or prescription drugs. Nutraceuticals' effect on the body is generally milder than that of pharmaceuticals. Consequently, they have fewer side effects but also take longer to achieve maximum results.

There is actually an extensive body of research attesting to the efficacy of these supplements in both humans and animals. Some of the safety studies for household pets are discussed later. But now, let's look at research on the effectiveness of glucosamine and chondroitin on horses. You may be wondering what horses' joint problems have to do with those of your miniature schnauzer. They have more in common than you might think. Although horses are much larger than the average house pet, they are not all that different in terms of skeletal structure. The fact that they weigh hundreds of pounds — and that many of them are quite active and continually stressing their joints with that weight — actually makes horses good "living laboratories" for the study of arthritis and its treatment.

When the injectable drug form of glucosamine and chondroitin sulfate (known as Adequan) was tested on horses, for example, it was found to increase the production of three elements required for healthy cartilage: collagen, hyaluronic acid, and proteoglycans.[34]

In the horse world these supplements are not news. Glucosamine and chondroitin sulfate supplements are widely used on both race- and show horses, for example, which are so valuable that preventing and curing osteoarthritis is a high priority. Consequently, owners, trainers, and the veterinarians have followed this treatment protocol closely. Today many stable managers routinely feed their horses these supplements. Even members of the U.S. Olympic equestrian team give oral glucosamine and chondroitin supplements (under the brand name Cosequin) to their mounts.

Considerable research has been conducted on horses. In a 1997 study conducted at Auburn University, for example, twenty-five horses with degenerative joint disease were treated with the glucosamine-chondroitin compound, Cosequin. The results were measured "pre" and "post" treatment, using several objective physical tests, including X rays of the affected joints. The researchers reported that "within two weeks . . . the lameness, flexion test, and stride length were significantly improved."[35]

In a double-blind, placebo-controlled study by the same research team, eight horses were fed Cosequin, while seven were given a placebo. The researchers concluded that there were substantial improvements in function and pain in the treated animals when compared with the placebo group.[36]

Proof from the Laboratories

The question remains, however, how relevant are horse studies to pets? We are happy to say that the answer is, very relevant. In fact, studies done with glucosamine and chondroitin in small animals have obtained similar results to those in human and horse research.

A clinical trial conducted in 1995 at the Department of Animal Biology at the University of Belgium investigated whether chondroitin supplements given orally to animals actually reach the target tissues of the cartilage. Researchers administered chondroitin sulfate to a test rat and dog, radioactively "labeling" the supplement so that they could trace it. Peak absorption into the plasma was observed within 1.6 hours for the rat, and 2.1 hours for the dog. Within twenty-four hours the supplement had concentrated in the synovial fluid, which "feeds" the cartilage, and the cartilage itself. And after thirty-six hours, the single dose of the supplements was still traceable in the animals' joints.[37]

Another study involving animals tested whether, once the supplement was absorbed, it was effective at reducing damaged cartilage. In this cooperative U.S./Swiss study, chymopapain (a product that induces a form of osteoarthritis) was injected into the left knee of twelve rabbits. The animals' right knees served as the control. Some of the animals were given chondroitin sulfate for ten days before the chymopapain injection, and continued receiving the supplement for twenty-one days afterward.

Eighty-four days later the animals' knees were examined. Of the animals that did not receive chondroitin sulfate, cartilage damage was 40 percent greater than in the control knee, which had not been affected by the injection. But cartilage damage in the rabbits taking the chondroitin sulfate was only 24 percent. Clearly, the chondroitin stopped a significant amount of the chemically induced cartilage loss. In fact, the results of this study suggest that glucosamine and chondroitin can be taken as preventatives, a nutritional form of insurance against developing arthritis. In medical terms, this makes them "chondroprotectives."[38]

Research on Pets

Glucosamine and chondroitin can be effectively employed to help minimize secondary osteoarthritis, which sometimes occurs as a result of injury and surgery. In a 1998 study of sixteen adult dogs that had surgical reconstruction of torn knee ligaments, eight dogs received Cosequin, while the others did not. The results showed that the dogs receiving the supplements suffered from 50 percent less osteoarthritis than the ones who did not. The glucosamine-chondroitin combination not only reduced the severity of the osteoarthritis in the operated joints, but the supplements returned the joints to a more normal, physiological joint capsule.[39]

In a study of thirteen dogs less than one year old, a glucosamine-chondroitin combination was administered for thirty days. According to the researchers, the data suggest that when orally administered, "levels of circulating agents which stimulate cartilage metabolism while inhibiting cartilage degradation" are elevated.[40]

Safety for Cats and Dogs

Although researchers have long known that glucosamine and chondroitin sulfate are safe for pets, this theory was put to the test for both groups of our furry friends.

Fifteen cats were evaluated for their adverse reaction to a glucosamine-chondroitin combination agent. Twelve of the cats received the agent, and the remaining three composed the control group. The researchers concluded that the use of the supplements posed no risk of clinically important blood, hemostatic (blood flow), or biochemical changes when given to cats over the thirty-day period.[41]

The same team conducted a similar study, this time on thirteen normal, healthy dogs. The treatment group consisted of ten dogs, and the control group, three. And again, the treatment lasted for thirty days. Although there were minor changes in the dogs' blood, hemostatic (blood flow), and biochemistry, none was clinically significant.[42]

More studies can be expected. The National Institutes of Health's Office of Alternative Medicine is now reviewing proposals for testing glucosamine and chondroitin sulfate through clinical trials. Meanwhile, it is clear that supplements of glucosamine and chondroitin sulfate have been extensively tested on animals, both small and large, with findings as impressive as those from human studies. As a result, more and more veterinarians are choosing them as the first line of treatment for pets with osteoarthritis.

In a survey of more than fifteen hundred veterinarians in the United States, for example, Cosequin was considered to be both safe and effective treatment for arthritis in dogs by more than 80 percent of the responding participants. "Good" to "excellent" results were noted by the veterinarians in regard to animal mobility (89 percent), alleviation of pain (83 percent), and improved attitude (85 percent).[43] Obviously, when it comes to treating osteoarthritis in pets, glucosamine and chondroitin are supplements whose time has come.

•   •   •

Now that we have established the effectiveness of the supplements that are part of the Arthritis Cure and have seen that they have been proved to be an invaluable means of restoring health to arthritic joints in humans and animals, the question is how they should be used. Like its predecessor, *The Arthritis Cure, The Arthritis Cure for Pets* relies on a protocol that revolves around these two remarkable substances, glucosamine and chondroitin sulfate. Keep in mind, however, that the most effective form of these supplements is glucosamine hydrochloride and purified chondroitin sulfate.

How to Use the Arthritis Cure Supplements for Pets

In Europe glucosamine is regulated and sold as the drug glucosamine sulfate. In this country glucosamine is available without a prescription. Of the four forms available, glucosamine hydrochloride is the one most often used in U.S. research. The effectiveness of other forms in reversing osteoarthritis, however, is not currently known.

The two primary forms of chondroitin are purified chondroitin sulfate

> **Over a period of time if an animal has osteoarthritis, the cartilage dries out as a result of the disease and eventually erodes, until it no longer functions as a buffer. An animal with joints in this condition can no longer enjoy pain-free movement.**

and mixed proteoglycans. It is important to remember that a low molecular weight, highly pure (95 percent) form of chondroitin sulfate is optimal. Glucosamine and chondroitin can be purchased as individual supplements or in combination form, from veterinary hospitals, pharmacies, health food stores, and supermarkets; on the Internet; and by mail order. But be aware that these supplements are marketed under various names and levels of purity. To ensure that a quality product is purchased, consult your veterinarian. Or if you have questions about glucosamine and chondroitin products, visit Brenda's web site at www.stayhealthy.com.

Before giving your pet any of these products, though, consult your veterinarian. Your pet should be examined and diagnosed with arthritis before receiving any medication, particularly since those not obtained from a veterinarian are intended for human use. Your veterinarian is likely to recommend a product designed specifically for pets. These range from injectable (Adequan) to oral supplements, such as Cosequin, PetJoint or Glyco-Flex (from Vetri-Science Laboratories) for dogs, or Nu-Cat (also from Vetri-Science) for cats. Other nutraceuticals, such as Super Oxide Dismutase (SOD; Gem State Nutrition), a blend of antioxidants for dogs and horses, might be included in the treatment regimen. In addition, pain relievers may be necessary for short-term relief, until the supplements reach maximum effectiveness; again, your veterinarian can recommend effective products as well as monitor any side effects.

Putting the Arthritis Cure to Work

Glucosamine and chondroitin sulfate supply the raw materials that can repair and restore damaged joints. In fact, they provide three unique aspects involved in the Arthritis Cure. First, glucosamine and chondroitin sulfate can actually repair and restore some of the damaged cartilage. Second, they prevent further degeneration. Third, they stimulate growth of new cartilage. In other words, glucosamine and chondroitin sulfate do much more than treat the symptoms. As damaged cartilage is restored to health, inflammation and pain are reduced, and even eliminated. With the ability to diminish or eliminate symptoms and restore the actual structure of joint tissues, glucosamine and chondroitin sulfate are indeed "chondroprotective agents."

These supplements are nearly always effective in inhibiting osteoarthritis and may be used in stopping the disease as well. But keep in mind that they are not miracle pills, able to cure all symptoms of the disease quickly and completely. Cartilage cannot be fully restored overnight. As you begin to treat your pet with these supplements, be sure to administer them for the full course of treatment, according to your veterinarian's instructions. By combining these supplements with the other components of the Six-Step Arthritis Cure for Pets Program discussed in the next chapter, you can maximize, and possibly even hasten, the results.

Next, you will learn how to rid your pet of arthritis, via the Six-Step Arthritis Cure for Pets Program. And in the chapters to come, we will show you how proper exercise, feeding, and vitamin and mineral supplements can combine to support your pet's health in regard to osteoarthritis, as well as other potentially devastating illnesses. This complete, health-enhancing program is designed to keep your cherished animals as happy and pain-free as possible, for as long as possible.

The Six-Step Arthritis Cure for Pets Program

Millions of pets suffer from osteoarthritis. For some it is an inconvenience. For others it is a debilitating and tragic experience. These pets do not have to suffer. As millions of human arthritis sufferers the world over have discovered, there is an alternative. In fact, using glucosamine and chondroitin sulfate and following the guidelines that make up the Six-Step Arthritis Cure for Pets can substantially relieve the symptoms of osteoarthritis. In many cases this dreaded disease can even be stopped and the damage reversed. And for pets that are healthy and free of osteoarthritis, using a modified version of this plan can help keep them that way.

Before looking at the plan in more detail, let's review what we know so far. We know that osteoarthritis is a degenerative disease affecting the cartilage in the joints. It can be caused by genetics, aging, injury, or excessive repetitive motions, which might occur in a chronic Frisbee chaser or a racing greyhound. Cats are less likely than dogs to develop the disease, simply because they carry less weight on their frames. By the same token, large dogs are more prone to developing osteoarthritis, because their joints carry more weight and therefore endure more stress. The older an animal is, the more likely it is to experience osteoarthritis, simply because of changes in joint tissues as a result of aging.

Regardless of its cause, osteoarthritis involves gradual disintegration of the cartilage, a tough, spongy substance that cushions the bones against the shock of daily activities. As the cartilage deteriorates, the joint lining, or synovium, becomes inflamed. The lining contains nerve endings and pain receptors that the cartilage does not have, so at this point, movement becomes painful. As the body tries to heal itself, the synovium steps up production of fluids. But this only leads to a swollen joint and even more pain. Eventually bones can become completely exposed, so that the ends rub against each other and become chipped and ragged. Bone spurs or bone fragments can lodge in the joint, making movement exceedingly painful.

Symptoms of the disease include difficulty rising from a sitting or lying position, stiffness of joints (particularly in the morning), limping or odd gaits, licking a joint, or sensitivity to being touched in the area of an arthritic joint. The difficulties created by osteoarthritis might also spawn such secondary symptoms as depression, withdrawal, antisocial behavior, aggression (especially when touched on the sore joint), whimpering or whining, and poor grooming. If the disease is not treated, the symptoms gradually become worse.

Traditionally, treating arthritis has involved painkillers, commonly known as nonsteroidal anti-inflammatory drugs, or NSAIDs. Unfortunately, while these pharmaceuticals may dampen the pain of the disease, they do nothing to improve the condition — and in some cases they even make it worse by causing further erosion of the cartilage.

Until recently veterinarians prescribed NSAIDs despite their drawbacks simply because there were no alternatives. That is no longer true. Double-blind studies from all over the world have provided ample proof that glucosamine and chondroitin sulfate — two safe, natural substances — can help rebuild the internal structure of damaged joint cartilage and restore it to its original, healthy state. Combining these two substances in a simple, easy-to-live-with program that supports their abilities is what the Six-Step Arthritis Cure for Pets is about — and it can make a dramatic difference in your pet's health.

Strategies for Minimizing the Effects of Joint Disease in House Pets and Larger Animals

In this book we are concerned with osteoarthritis and ways to minimize its symptoms in pets. Research has shown that by approaching the disease from several different angles, it is possible to reduce the symptoms, restore cartilage, and in some cases even cure the disease. In order to do so, the pet owner needs to follow the Six-Step Arthritis Cure for Pets Program:

1. Have your pet properly diagnosed by a veterinarian.
2. Use glucosamine and chondroitin sulfate with their nutritional supplement enhancers.
3. Take advantage of painkillers — temporarily.
4. Exercise your pet regularly.
5. Avoid injury, and quickly attend to injuries if they do occur.
6. Follow the Arthritis Cure for Pets Feeding Plan.

Step 1: Have Your Pet Properly Diagnosed by a Veterinarian

Anyone who has ever gone through the frustration of having a health problem misdiagnosed knows that it is not a pleasant experience. The same is true for animals. Not all joint problems are caused by osteoarthritis. Treating a pet with the Six-Step Arthritis Cure for Pets Program because you assume it has this disease is a serious mistake. You may end up giving an animal medication and supplements that will not help its condition at all. Worse, you are delaying access to medicine that will improve its health. Your veterinarian can conduct a complete physical examination and conduct the necessary tests to determine your pet's overall health and the source of any joint problems. Only on a professional's recommendation should you begin this program. And if your veterinarian is skeptical or even against this program, find a veterinary professional who is receptive.

The only exception to this rule is for those who would like to prevent osteoarthritis from developing in their pets. However, a veterinarian should still give your pet a complete physical to rule out the disease, so that you will know whether to follow our Six-Step Arthritis Cure for Pets Program or the preventative plan.

Step 2: Use Glucosamine and Chondroitin Sulfate and Their Nutritional Supplement Enhancers

In many ways the most important part of the Six-Step Arthritis Cure for Pets Program is to give your pet supplements to ensure a healthy and full life expectancy. These days many animals are stricken by the same degenerative diseases that afflict humans. Cases of cancer and arthritis are on the rise as animals are subjected to diets of poor quality and the environmental toxins we all live with.

Glucosamine and chondroitin sulfate, enhanced by other nutritional supplements and herbs, can make a major difference in the health of joint tissues when given consistently. A multivitamin/mineral supplement in powdered form can easily be added to your pet's food. The supplement should include antioxidant vitamins and minerals to help protect bone joints from deterioration. In addition, many quality pet foods are adding nutritional supplements to their mixtures. Check to see if yours is one. Chapter 6 outlines the appropriate combination of vitamins and minerals that enhance the Six-Step Arthritis Cure for Pets Program. Keep in mind that although vitamin supplements are important to boost your pet's health, only glucosamine and chondroitin sulfate can stop, reverse, or even cure your pet's osteoarthritis.

Dosage

Cosequin, the combination product used in most U.S. research studies on pets and by the majority of veterinarians, recommends the following dosage levels:

Cats and small dogs: Cosequin Regular Strength (250 mg glucosamine hydrochloride; 200 mg chondroitin sulfate; 33 mg manganese ascorbate)

Initial administration: four to six weeks

Under 10 pounds: ½ to 1 capsule daily
10–24 pounds: 2 capsules daily

Maintenance administration: six weeks plus

Under 10 pounds: ½ capsule daily, or 1 capsule every other day
10–24 pounds: 1 capsule daily

Medium and large dogs: Cosequin Double Strength (500 mg glucosamine hydrochloride; 400 mg chondroitin sulfate; 66 mg manganese ascorbate)
Initial administration: four to six weeks

25–49 pounds: 2 capsules daily, 1 in the A.M., 1 in the P.M.
50–100 pounds: 3 capsules daily; 2 in the A.M., 1 in the P.M.
Over 100 pounds: 4 capsules daily; 2 in the A.M., 2 in the P.M.

Maintenance administration: six weeks plus

25–49 pounds: dosage is lowered in increments of ½ capsule per month
50+ pounds: dosage is lowered in increments of 1 capsule per month

Enhancers to Glucosamine and Chondroitin

Alternative treatments like acupuncture, chiropractic, massage, and herbal remedies are a few of the time-honored treatments that may also promote joint health. You may have to experiment to determine which work best for your pet, but it is time well spent. Knowing that you have finally discovered the magic bullet that eases your pet's pain is a truly joyful moment. Chapter 8 reviews other treatments that can enhance the Six-Step Arthritis Cure for Pets Program.

Step 3:   Take Advantage of Painkillers — Temporarily

As noted, painkillers like NSAIDs can be both a blessing and a curse. They are part of the Six-Step Arthritis Cure for Pets Program because, when used for short-term pain relief, they accomplish their goal. Like herbs and other natural remedies, glucosamine and chondroitin sulfate do not produce the virtually instant results that can be obtained with pharmaceuticals. Studies have shown that it may take anywhere from two weeks to a month for these supplements to provide pain relief. In the meantime, using veterinarian-recommended or -prescribed painkillers allows your pet to get the exercise it needs to strengthen the joint and nourish the cartilage.

When you and your veterinarian determine that it is time to stop the painkillers, do so gradually. Your veterinarian can explain how to reduce the amount of these drugs your pet is taking in such a way that its system has time to adjust.

Step 4: Exercise Your Pet Regularly

Just as humans become stiff and lame without exercise, a sedentary animal will develop awkward and unnatural movements as well. It is vital that an animal be exercised every day. Movement keeps joints lubricated, nourished, and free of toxins. It also builds strong muscles, tendons, and ligaments that support joints and absorb stress that might otherwise damage cartilage and neighboring tissues.

Aerobic exercise — brisk walking, jogging, hiking — provides extra oxygen and builds stamina. But you can also accomplish the other two exercise essentials, stretching and strength training, with aerobics. A dog that leaps for a ball, for example, is stretching. And running up stairs or the slope of a hill is a fine method of strength training. Indoor house pets deserve adequate and appropriate exercise too. Taking the effort to make some space and provide appropriate toys is all it takes to enable an indoor pet to flex muscles and bend joints sufficiently each day.

It is always best to exercise for several short sessions during the day rather than once a day for a long period of time. As

muscles fatigue with strenuous exercise, more impact is transmitted to the joint, which results in increased pain and other arthritis
symptoms. Chapter 9 takes a more in-depth look at how exercise
can help your pet's recovery from osteoarthritis.

Step 5:   Avoid Injury, and Quickly Attend to Injuries if They Do Occur

Dog owners who live in a crowded metropolitan area need to
keep a watchful eye — as well as a leash, unless you have access
to a leash-free park — on their dogs when they exercise. Of
course, the same is true in suburban neighborhoods and even in
the country. All too many dogs are struck by vehicles each year,
receiving severe, and sometimes fatal, injuries.

If you have a cat, go through your house as you would if you
had a toddler, looking for furnishings and structures that could
potentially harm your feline friend. There may be a cabinet that
could tip over easily or a television set too close to the edge of a
shelf. Many veterinarians suggest keeping a cat indoors, at least at
night, when coyotes and other predators roam.

Finally, while it's always exciting to see your animal "perform"
some amazing stunt — and some four-legged show-offs are all
too happy to do so — putting an animal in danger by coaxing it
into risky feats can lead to injury. Use common sense, and leave
the circus acts for the professionals.

Caring for Injuries Properly

Muscle damage: If an animal strains or sprains a muscle, the
RICE (rest, ice, compress, elevate) procedure mentioned earlier
is the best way to prevent the problem from getting worse. If a
muscle or tendon is injured, apply ice immediately to the injured
area, to reduce swelling and inflammation. Do not lay ice directly
on an animal's body. Lay a sock or a thin towel on your pet first,

then place the ice on top. Keep the area iced for twenty minutes at a time, three times a day.

In the first stages of healing, wrapping the affected area in a compress, such as an Ace bandage, reduces inflammation. Be careful not to wrap the bandage so tightly that you can't get your finger between it and your pet's body, or you may restrict circulation and do further damage.

Rest is the third component of the RICE procedure, so try to keep your pet as quiet as possible, until pain and inflammation are under control, and rehabilitation can begin. Elevation is the final component of RICE, but we recognize that elevating an animal's sore limb just may not be possible without causing it undue stress. If your dog or cat doesn't mind resting its leg on a pillow, fine. If not, don't make an issue of it. Since you know your pet best, we leave that decision up to you.

Following the RICE procedures lessens recovery time. If the injury involves tissues of the joint, these steps can also reduce the chances of the injured animal's developing related osteoarthritis later in life.

Fracture: If an animal has a fractured limb, the leg will "bend" at a sharp angle and the animal will not use the leg. Take your pet to a veterinarian immediately. Do not try to temporarily stabilize the limb with a splint. Animals often struggle during attempts to splint the leg, which could lead to the bone perforating the skin. Instead, simply put your pet carefully in the car and go to the veterinarian as soon as possible. If the skin is broken at the fracture, gently cover it with clean gauze and tape.

A padded box works well for transporting small animals. A larger dog, though, may have to walk on three legs or be carried, if possible. These efforts can spare your pet more distress and further minimize damage to joint tissue, so they are well worth it.

Step 6:   Follow the Arthritis Cure for Pets Feeding Plan

An anti-osteoarthritic diet can benefit your pet. New commercial foods are being produced that contain ingredients such as glucosamine, chondroitin sulfate, and omega-3 fatty acids, which may help prevent or decrease symptoms associated with osteoarthritis. If you choose commercial pet foods, check that the food is fresh and the expiration date has not been passed, because fats within the food can become rancid and affect an animal's health. Many excellent commercial foods, such as Iams, Hills, Waltham, and Purina, are available from your veterinarian and pet supply store. And if you have the time and interest, home-cooked foods ensure freshness and are very nutritious, as long as they contain a proper balance of nutrients.

Pets should be fed at the same time each day, normally once in the morning and once at night. If you are feeding your pet wet food, any food not eaten after half an hour should be thrown away. This prevents your pet from eating food that has been contaminated by bacteria.

Crunchy nibbles between meals, such as homemade snacks or raw vegetables, are fine in moderation. In fact, you may be surprised at your pet's response to a healthy snack. A friend's dog, who initially turned his nose up at the sight of a carrot, now gleefully chews it with the enthusiasm once reserved only for marrow bones. Be careful when choosing commercial pet nibbles, biscuits, and "treats"— some brands contain high levels of sugar and salt, while others are nutritionally sound.

> On the Arthritis Cure for Pets Feeding Plan, an animal will also enjoy a higher level of energy, a healthier-looking coat, and be in good spirits.

Ingredients for a Healthy Pet's Diet

You know your pet better than anyone else does, so it only makes sense for you to be the one to select the foods for the home-cooked meals. So instead of recipes, we have included lists of appropriate ingredients, along with suggested amounts, that you can mix and match according to your pet's preferences.

Meats: Since dogs and cats are carnivores, meat plays an essential role in their diet and should be one of the main ingredients in any homemade pet food (about 50 percent). Since animals in the wild usually do not eat only one food, it's best to vary the meats you choose. Most meats can be fed raw, but fish, rabbit, and pork should be cooked to kill any parasites. Also, feed raw liver sparingly. It should not be more than 10 percent of the meat content in any meal you make for your pet, because of its high content of saturated fats. Here are some suggestions:

Skinless turkey (with or without giblets)
Skinless chicken (with or without giblets)
Liver or heart (from turkey, beef, or chicken)
Lean ground beef
Lamb
Brains
Chuck or sirloin steak
Duck
Tuna and other fish
Rabbit

The other proteins: Among the protein-rich foods that can be included in a pet's diet are eggs and dairy products (choose non- or low-fat) such as cottage cheese, milk, and yogurt. Ask your veterinarian about the risk of raw eggs versus cooked eggs. Not all experts agree that dogs and cats can digest eggs or dairy products well. If after feeding a pet one of these foods, you notice any signs of upset stomach, such as vomiting or diarrhea, discontinue the practice.

Grains and more: Grains, beans, and legumes are great sources of carbohydrates and can also supply complete protein when combined. Although meat should be served raw, grains need to be cooked so that your pet can digest them. Choose from:

Rice, either brown or white (white rice can be binding and cause constipation in some animals, but it is highly digestible)

Barley

Cornmeal

Millet

Whole wheat (whole wheat bread is fine)

Rolled oats

Bulgur

Lentils

Split peas

Navy, black, red, or pinto beans

Vegetables: Try adding one or more of these cooked veggies to your pet's meal:

Broccoli

Corn

Peas

Green beans

Carrots (if your pet likes them raw, give them to your pet as a snack)

Potatoes

Raw parsley and zucchini (grated or finely chopped) can be mixed in, too.

Supplementing the Diet

When looking for a multivitamin and mineral supplement for your pet, make sure the product you choose contains the elements listed below. Keep in mind that pets have different nutritional requirements than humans — so buy supplements that are specifically formulated for pets. And be sure to talk with your veterinarian about the most appropriate amount for your pet.

Antioxidants A, C, and E

B-complex vitamins

Calcium

Selenium

Other ingredients that make up a healthy meal include bonemeal (available as powder in health food stores) and cold-pressed vegetable oil (corn, safflower, or canola).

Putting It All Together

Here are a couple of easy homemade meals that incorporate many of the healthful ingredients we've discussed. The first recipe has been adapted from the book *Natural Dog Care,* by Dr. Bruce Fogle:

Easy Doggie Dinner

¾ cup brown rice

1 tbsp. bonemeal

⅓ tsp. corn or sunflower oil

Pinch of iodized salt

2 oz. skinless, cooked, diced chicken or turkey, or beef

½ cup cooked, chopped peas, carrots, or other vegetable

Cook the brown rice, bonemeal, oil, and salt for 30 minutes, using twice as much water as the package directions recommend. (This softens the rice and makes it more digestible, since dogs sometimes have a hard time digesting grains). Cool the rice mixture, then stir in the chopped vegetables and meat.

This amount feeds an active, twenty-two-pound dog for one day, so adjust the amount according to the weight and activity level of your pet.

The next recipe has been adapted from *Dr. Pitcairn's Complete Guide to Natural Health for Dogs and Cats:*

Quick Kitty Delight

1 cup cooked meat (skinless chicken or turkey, beef, or fish)

1½ tsp. bonemeal

1 tsp. finely chopped or pureed cooked peas or other vegetable (optional)

1 egg, beaten (optional)

Chop the cooked meat and stir in the bonemeal and vegetables or egg, if desired.

Maintaining Normal Weight

Consult your veterinarian to determine the ideal body-weight range for your pet. He or she can assign a body condition score to your pet that can be monitored over time to optimize joint function and minimize progression of osteoarthritis. Being overweight stresses the joints and can even change the surface and interior structure of the joint, inviting the first stages of osteo-arthritis. Pets with early stages of arthritis begin to show signs of pain and lethargy if they become overweight.

If you put your pet on a diet, serve reduced portions of a nutritious, lower-calorie food. The best foods provide animals with essential nutrients, such as vitamin B_6 and flavonoids. Inadequate amounts of these substances can lead to osteoarthritis.

> **Be careful not to feed your pet high-calorie dog cookies — in some instances these products contain so much sugar, you might as well be feeding them candy bars!**

While your pet is on a weight-loss program, give it nutritional supplements. Consult your veterinarian for advice on low-calorie pet foods, proper supplements, and a healthy rate of weight loss. Once the desired weight is reached, it is your responsibility to help your pet maintain it. So don't return to the earlier feeding habits that caused weight gain in the first place. Weigh your pet weekly and keep a record of the weight so you can easily tell when it's time to increase or decrease food.

The Power of a Preventive Program

One of the most exciting aspects of the Six-Step Arthritis Cure for Pets Program is that you don't have to wait until your dog or cat actually has arthritis to put it to work for you. In other words, providing any animal — whether it is young or simply lucky enough to be free of the disease — with four out of the six steps can help prevent osteoarthritis from developing.

To employ the preventive approach, take the following four steps:

1. Consult with your veterinarian to make certain your pet's joints are healthy.

2. Exercise your pet regularly.
3. Avoid injury, and quickly attend to injuries if they do occur.
4. Follow the Arthritis Cure for Pets Feeding Plan.

If signs of arthritis eventually appear, schedule a trip to the veterinarian for a professional diagnosis. Then follow the complete six-step program for minimizing symptoms as outlined earlier.

> *Les and Carolyn created their own version of the Six-Step Arthritis Cure for Pets Program accidentally, when their gorgeous golden retriever pup, Boots, was hit by a car before her first birthday. At first, Les and Carolyn were glad she was alive, and her broken leg healed nicely. But a few years later Carolyn noticed that Boots had trouble getting up. She attributed it to their slippery hardwood floors and placed a few area rugs in strategic places. Then while letting Boots run at the park, Les noticed that her gait was awkward.*
>
> *At the veterinarian, X rays showed osteoarthritis in Boots's right hip joint, no doubt a result of the accident. Surgery was discussed as an option, but before the operation, the orthopedic surgeon sat Les and Carolyn down for a "little talk." Boots, he said, will likely have a higher chance of complication with surgery because of damage that occurred when she was a puppy. He suggested they think it over before opting for an operation, with its own risks, even though the long-term prognosis was poor in terms of joint health. Adept at reading between the lines, Les and Carolyn knew he was suggesting they put Boots down and get a new dog. But neither one was interested. They had never had children, and in the few years they'd spent with Boots, she had stolen their hearts*

with her intelligence and devotion. They vowed to do everything possible to make her life long and happy.

After reading dozens of books on arthritis and talking to their own doctors about it, Les and Carolyn made changes in Boots's diet, adding raw meat and vegetables to high-grade kibble. They sought out a vitamin-mineral supplement that provided antioxidants and essential trace minerals. After they discovered that exercise was highly recommended for arthritis patients, Boots began going on short walks three times a day and was taken to a nearby lake on the weekends for a swim, weather permitting. In the evenings, when Boots lay at the foot of their bed, Les and Carolyn would take turns massaging her, giving her hip extra but gentle attention. Then they heard about glucosamine and chondroitin sulfate supplements and added those to Boots's daily regimen. A few months later, during a routine visit to the veterinarian, he asked about Boots's hip. When he saw her walk without a limp, he was impressed. The veterinarian claimed it was a miracle — but Les and Carolyn knew it was actually the result of the changes they had made. But the truth was, they didn't care. They had achieved their goal of keeping Boots healthy and happy for as long as possible, and that was what really mattered.

New Discoveries in Vitamins and Minerals

Although vitamins were discovered almost a hundred years ago, scientists are only now learning how powerful they are to maintaining good health. In fact, it sometimes seems that new studies telling us why we should take vitamins are released every week. Unfortunately, studies explaining why vitamins may be bad for our health come along at about the same frequency. Trying to keep up with the latest studies and trends can be a mind-boggling experience. Even medical experts don't agree on which vitamins — if any — are necessary for optimal health. For the average consumer, sorting through the conflicting information can be frustrating, at best. The situation isn't much easier for those of us whose livelihood depends on being aware of the latest research in nutrition and health. But as health experts, we have observed that certain theories regarding vitamins and minerals are becoming more widely accepted.

One such major movement is toward greater acceptance of regular vitamin and mineral supplementation. In the past many doctors considered vitamin supplements a waste of time. "Eat a balanced diet," they encouraged their patients. "You'll get all the vitamins you need from that." Today, however, more and more physicians recommend that their patients take supplements. And although nutrition experts still insist that the best source of vitamins and minerals is food, most agree that it is difficult for even the most conscientious eaters to eat balanced meals consistently.

Another strong case for supplements is the fact that antioxidants are becoming considered a cornerstone of good health. Although some medical experts still find them controversial, antioxidants continue to prove their value in study after study. There are a variety of antioxidants, but the "big four" are vitamins A (in the form of beta-carotene), C, and E and the mineral selenium, conveniently distilled to the acronym ACES.

So far, we have been talking about developments in human health. But much of what scientists have learned about vitamins and minerals applies to pets as well. Dogs, cats, horses, and other mammals also require vitamins to keep their cells healthy and their bodies functioning. Their precise needs are somewhat different from ours, of course, and those differences are discussed in more depth shortly. First, let's look at one important way our vitamin and mineral needs are similar to those of our pets'— and that is in regard to joint degeneration.

• • •

Researchers are discovering that certain substances in foods can affect joint deterioration by slowing or halting the accompanying inflammation. Therefore, supplementing your pet's diet with substances that prevent degeneration — as well as feeding it foods containing beneficial substances — can have a profound impact on a pet's joint health. (This is as true for humans as it is for animals, so you may want to incorporate some of these supplements into your diet, after consulting your physician.)

Take, for example, the role of antioxidants. According to the prevailing theory, antioxidants are essential for good health because they stabilize "free radicals," unsteady molecules that have either lost an electron or are saddled with extras. Pollution, medication, stress, sunlight, X rays, some foods and beverages, and even intense exercise can create free radicals. They are also the by-products of chemical reactions with oxygen that occur within the body. The joint inflammation that can accompany osteoarthritis can lead to an increased rate of free-radical production. These damaged molecules wander through our bodies, stealing electrons from other molecules in an attempt to restore their balance. The problem is that when the free radicals take electrons from healthy tissue, they damage it in the process. Unstable oxygen molecules — called singlet oxygen, because there is only one oxygen molecule instead of the usual pair — are among the most damaging of the free radicals. Oxidation doesn't occur just in the body, of course. When a piece of metal darkens or deteriorates, for example, or a tin can rusts, oxidation is responsible.

> In the case of osteoarthritis, limiting the formation of free radicals is a critical part of any prevention or treatment plan.

Everything from aging and cancer to heart disease and other degenerative conditions has been linked to free radicals. Studies have shown that free radicals can damage key components of cartilage, including the proteoglycans and collagen, while accelerating the course of the disease. And this means that antioxidants — which bind with free radicals in singlet oxygen to make them stable again — are an essential means of dealing with the disease.

Proof of this process, at least in humans, was well established with the famous Framingham Heart Study, which involved 640 residents of Framingham, Massachusetts. Although the focus of the research was cardiac disease, the scientists also explored the origins of other health problems, including osteoarthritis. During two physical exams spaced ten years apart, participants were examined for symptoms of knee osteoarthritis. The subjects also completed food-intake questionnaires. The researchers then correlated the incidence of osteoarthritis of the knee with intake of various antioxidants, including vitamin E, beta-carotene, and vitamin C. Results showed that antioxidants in general were protective, and that vitamin C was especially beneficial in helping to prevent osteoarthritis.[44]

Scientific Evidence from the Animal Kingdom

A randomized, double-blind study, appearing in the April 1998 issue of the *Veterinary Quarterly*, demonstrates that antioxidant therapy can help treat osteoarthritis. Eighteen dogs between the ages of one and thirteen were diagnosed with osteoarthritis secondary to canine hip dysplasia. Treatment consisted of giving one group of the dogs a multivitamin antioxidant, Proanthozone. The other group of dogs did not receive any treatment.

At the beginning of the study, the animals were assessed for lameness and range of motion in each coxofemoral joint (also known as the hip joint), and the owners of these animals also assessed the dogs' functional ability at two-week intervals throughout the study. The researchers found that those dogs treated with the antioxidant supplement showed significant clinical improvement.[45]

The researchers theorize that joint laxity, or looseness of the joint, which is considered a prime cause of hip dysplasia, may trigger the release of free radicals into the joint. These unstable molecules then damage joint and connective tissue sufficiently to create the joint pain and inflammation we know as osteoarthritis. Antioxidants are effective in treating the condition, because these nutrients bind with, and thereby disable, free radicals.

The Anti-Arthritis Team

As effective as glucosamine and chondroitin sulfate may be in treating osteoarthritis in your pet, antioxidants and other supplements can work with these compounds to maximize their benefits. These are vitamins and minerals found in everyday foods and in nutritional supplements. In fact, many are probably substances you take yourself. While food is frequently considered the best source of vitamins and minerals, it is not always possible to get a pet to eat some of the richest sources. Chapter 5 details some food ingredients that can be used as building blocks to create healthful meals. We realize that for many people, though, making pet food at home simply is not possible. Ask your veterinarian to recommend a good all-purpose dog or cat multivitamin and mineral supplement. Most of these products are very tasty, and pets eat them without hesitation. Remember that dogs and cats should not be given vitamins that are intended for humans unless you are doing so under the supervision of a veterinarian. Similarly, do not give cat supplements to your dog. The two animals have different nutritional needs and supplement requirements. In fact, it's not even a good idea to feed cat food to a dog, or vice versa.

Before looking at specific nutrients, it is important to distinguish between the two categories of vitamins, known as water-soluble and fat-soluble. The fat-soluble group, which includes vitamins A, D, E, and K, can be stored in the body, which is why an excess of them can be toxic, to both animals and humans.

Water-soluble vitamins, on the other hand, are stored less efficiently in the body. Excess amounts are removed through urination, so these vitamins are less likely to have toxic effects. But because they are not stored, they have to be ingested regularly. The B-complex of vitamins as well as vitamin C are in this group.

Vitamin A, Beta-Carotene, and the Carotenoids

The form of vitamin A found in plants, known as beta-carotene, is a powerful antioxidant. Beta-carotene is part of a large group of compounds called carotenoids, considered by some experts to be the most important dietary antioxidants. There are more than four hundred carotenoids, but only thirty to fifty have vitamin A activity. When these special carotenoids are ingested, the body converts them to vitamin A. (True vitamin A is also available in animal foods.)

Carotenoids are naturally occurring pigments, the most widespread in nature. They are easily identified by their characteristic yellow-orange hue, the color of carrots and winter squash.

Because many different carotenoids have antioxidant activity, food that naturally contains a range of these substances is the best source of carotene. Sweet potatoes, yams, carrots, cooked peas, broccoli, and green leafy vegetables such as raw parsley (the green of chlorophyll in leafy vegetables overrides the orange pigment of the carotenoids) all contain large amounts. Other sources include raw alfalfa sprouts and green beans.

Vitamin C

In nutritional studies conducted shortly after World War II, scientists discovered that animals have the unique ability to produce vitamin C in their own body tissues. Dogs, however, produce relatively small amounts of vitamin C compared with cats and other small mammals. So part of the treatment of osteoarthritis in pets involves combining vitamin C (often in the form of manganese ascorbate) with glucosamine and chondroitin. Preliminary scientific evidence shows that manganese ascorbate can stimulate the production of proteoglycans.

About Vitamin C

Vitamin C, also known as ascorbic acid, is the most unstable of vitamins. Its potency is lost when it is exposed to light, heat, and especially oxygen. Most of us think of vitamin C as something to take when we feel a cold coming on. And certainly vitamin C has been proved to support the immune system, helping the body fight bacterial infections and even reducing the effects of some allergy-producing substances. But vitamin C has a long list of other, less well known responsibilities. One of its primary roles in the body is to help maintain and build collagen, the structural fibers found in cartilage and the most abundant protein in the body. But vitamin C is essential for healthy bones as well as healthy joints; indeed, the two are intimately related. Bones are not simply composed of minerals, although you might think so, since calcium has received so much attention when it comes to keeping bones strong. In fact, collagen, a primary ingredient in cartilage, is also a component of bone, where it is found in a non-mineral matrix of other proteins. A vitamin C deficiency is associated with retarded bone calcification and bone matrix formation.

In addition to playing a role in the structure of bones, vitamin C affects joint health in other ways. Since it is one of the water-soluble vitamins, vitamin C can enter the interior of joints, where synovial fluid is stored. Here vitamin C works as an antioxidant, helping to preserve joint tissues from free radicals.

Studies with humans have shown another way that vitamin C helps treat arthritis is by strengthening the capillary walls in the joints: vitamin C prevents the capillaries from breaking down. If capillary walls are destroyed, bleeding, swelling, and pain can result. A number of studies with animals have confirmed vitamin C's potential as part of a comprehensive arthritis treatment plan. In one study, for example, researchers examined the importance of vitamin C in guinea pigs with induced osteoarthritis. They found that those animals that had received high doses of vitamin C had much less erosion of cartilage, and that overall changes in and around the osteoarthritic joints were milder.[46]

> Commercial pet food is an unlikely source of vitamin C, which is very fragile and easily destroyed by cooking and processing.

Researchers have also found that vitamin C supports the work of glucosamine and chondroitin sulfate supplements in another way. In animal studies, a vitamin C deficiency resulted in slower production of proteoglycans, which, as we have seen, are one of the main components of cartilage. It is likely that vitamin C supplements increase proteoglycans production, enhancing the effectiveness of the Arthritis Cure.[47]

Meanwhile, another study found that extra vitamin C was essential for the synthesis of protein for chondrocytes, the tiny factories that produce new collagen and proteoglycan molecules.[48] And research with elderly people has supported these findings, concluding that vitamin C deficiency results in altered collagen synthesis and compromised connective tissue repair.[49]

Vitamin C and Other Vitamins Function Synergistically

Although vitamin C is an excellent choice for enhancing the effectiveness of the Six-Step Arthritis Cure for Pets Program, there are two other vitamins that work in synergy with vitamin C to "enhance the enhancer," you might say.

For example, researchers know that while vitamin C is essential for creating the bone framework in most mammals, it is vitamin D that mineralizes bone once it is created. That is why milk and some other dairy products are fortified with vitamin D, for maximum benefit to the bones.

As an antioxidant, vitamin C also helps prevent other vitamins from being oxidized. These include two fat-soluble vitamins, vitamins A and E, and the water-soluble B vitamins thiamin, riboflavin, folic acid, and pantothenic acid, all of which are important to liver function and the elimination of toxins from the system.

Recent research has also shed light on the role of vitamin E in relation to vitamin C in cartilage health. When taken together, these vitamins appear to increase the stability of proteoglycans, those water-loving molecules that are so essential to healthy joint cartilage.[50] Vitamin E is discussed in more depth shortly.

Giving Your Pet Vitamin C Supplements

Even though animals are able to make their own vitamin C, we have no way of knowing whether they are producing sufficient quantities, especially when it comes to fighting disease. As a result, supplements are recommended, particularly for a pet with osteoarthritis.

Below are suggested dosages as a treatment plan for arthritis. Consult with your veterinarian if you have questions.

Preventive dosage for dogs: For prevention, giving an animal vitamin C supplements can help minimize and prevent osteoarthritis. A pet, depending on its size, can be given from 100 to 1,000 mg of vitamin C per day. Small dogs, such as a Pekinese or a puppy, need 100 mg; a large puppy, such as a German shepherd, 250 to 500 mg; 500 to 800 mg for most sizes of mature dogs; and as much as 1,000 mg for giant breeds such as Saint Bernard and Great Dane.

Dosage for treating arthritis in dogs: As a treatment, use 500 to 2,000 mg dosages, divided in half and given twice daily, with meals. This method maximizes absorption, since this water-soluble nutrient is not stored in the body and is usually eliminated in three to four hours. One way to tell if your dog is getting too much vitamin C is to observe its stools. If the stool becomes softer than normal, the dose of vitamin C should be reduced at least temporarily. A gradual increase in dose can be attempted later.

Cats and vitamin C: Many veterinarians recommend vitamin C for cats with osteoarthritis. For a fifteen-pound cat, the suggested dosage at the beginning of treatment is 200 mg per day, divided into two equal doses of 100 mg. Decrease the amount as the symptoms improve, until you reach a satisfactory maintenance dosage. The exact amount will vary, depending on your cat's overall health. Of course, vitamins A, the B complex, D, and E are also recommended; so again, we suggest having the veterinarian select an appropriate multivitamin-mineral formula for the sake of balance. If possible, purchase a multivitamin-mineral powder that can be mixed into your cat's favorite food. Digesting a whole vitamin pill can be difficult for some cats, especially seniors with less-active digestive systems.

Vitamin E

Vitamin E is a fat-soluble vitamin made up of compounds called tocopherols. There are seven naturally occurring forms of tocopherols, but the one that has the most nutritional value and is the most potent is alpha-tocopherol. The others, such as beta, gamma, and delta, are called "mixed tocopherols" and are sometimes included in vitamin E supplements.

The best way to give an animal the benefit of natural vitamin E is through whole foods. The most concentrated sources of tocopherols are cold-pressed vegetable oils (such as sunflower and safflower), nuts, soybeans, and raw whole seeds, like sunflower. Vitamin E supplements are also available in capsules.

> Various substances can destroy vitamin E, including rancid oil or fat, inorganic iron compounds, and the chlorine in drinking water.

Although natural vitamin E, labeled as d-alpha tocopherol, is more effective in humans than the synthetic form (dl-alpha tocopherol), it is not known whether the same is true for animals. To be on the safe side, if your veterinarian recommends vitamin E in supplement form, use the natural version.

Vitamin E has an impressive résumé as an antioxidant. First, it helps prevent vitamin A and saturated fatty acids from breaking down, thereby halting the formation of free radicals. It also prevents oxidation of vitamin C and the B-complex vitamins. Vitamin E may play a role in calcium metabolism too, by helping regulate the deposits of this mineral to areas that need it most.

Flavonoids: A Partner to Vitamin C

In order for the body to metabolize vitamin C and make use of other nutrients, flavonoids must be present. These are a large class of nutrient (more than four thousand different types) and are found in virtually all foods. Like the carotenoids, flavonoids are plant pigments, contributing the coloring of most fruits and flowers.

> If a joint is injured, which can set the stage for the development of osteoarthritis, flavonoids can speed the healing process.

Flavonoids offer exceptional protection against a wide range of different free radicals. They can slow the progress of osteoarthritis and help reverse the disease, by

- helping collagen form a strong matrix
- limiting damage to tissues by free radicals
- decreasing inflammation
- preserving collagen and preventing it from being destroyed when joint tissue is inflamed
- helping injuries heal more rapidly

Food sources for flavonoids include fresh fruits and vegetables, whole grains, and seeds. Citrus, berries, onions, and green tea contain the highest concentration of these nutrients. Of course, most animals have no interest in these foods, but a good supplement should provide all the necessary flavonoids. As always, talk with your veterinarian before giving your pet flavonoids.

Vitamin D

Recent studies have shown that vitamin D plays a role in preventing osteoarthritis. In testing whether the recommended daily allowance for humans (200 IU) was sufficient to prevent osteoarthritis, researchers at the Arthritis Center at Boston University Medical Center found that people taking double this amount had a lower risk of developing joint disease and arthritis.

Food sources of vitamin D include egg yolk, yeast, and cod liver oil. It is also added to milk if the label says "fortified" with vitamin D. The body naturally converts sunlight into vitamin D, too, so most animals presumably are not deficient. But housebound pets, such as cats living in apartments or dogs that spend most of their time indoors, may be lacking in this essential vitamin. Be aware, though, that vitamin D can be toxic. Before supplementing your pet's diet, consult your veterinarian.

> An animal that is rarely exposed to sunlight may require foods that provide vitamin D.

Vitamin D helps stabilize joints and the bones surrounding weight-bearing joints. Stronger bones, of course, reduce stress on the joint and take weight off ligaments and cartilage. The quality of the bone directly underneath the cartilage (called the subchondral bone) must be adequate to support the cartilage and maintain its health. Studies focusing on knee joints show that vitamin D supplements keep cartilage in the knee area healthier. The vitamin may also slow cartilage degeneration with its antioxidant abilities.

Minerals That Support the Arthritis Cure for Pets

Minerals maintain healthy body chemistry and fluid balance, as well as regulate the formation of bone and other tissues in the body. Many animal-health experts believe that popular pet foods lack the minerals dogs and cats need; others feel that the better grades of commercial pet foods are fine. Giving your pet mineral supplements is not a decision you should make on your own. But if your veterinarian suggests supplements, remember that minerals cannot be given haphazardly. While the body easily eliminates excess vitamin C, for example, the same is not true of minerals. High doses of minerals are never recommended. In addition, most minerals work synergistically with vitamins and other minerals, so they should be taken together and in certain amounts. A proper balance of vitamins and minerals is the key. Generally, pet vitamin formulas contain vitamins and minerals in appropriate and balanced amounts. Supplementing a pet's diet with only one substance can create body-chemistry problems. Consult your veterinarian before adding specific individual mineral supplements to any animal's diet.

Minerals fall into two classifications — macro and micro — depending on how much of the specific nutrient is found in the body. Macro minerals for dogs include carbon, calcium, magnesium, phosphorous, potassium, silicon, sodium chloride, and sulfur. Micro minerals include chromium, cobalt, copper, fluoride, iodine, iron, manganese, molybdenum, selenium, strontium, tin, vanadium, and zinc.

For cats, the ash in commercial cat food generally provides all the necessary minerals. Beware of foods that contain amounts of ash in excess of 4 percent in canned foods and 12 percent in dry food. Beyond these safe amounts, ash can create a variety of health problems.

When it comes to augmenting the Arthritis Cure for Pets, two minerals stand out — manganese and selenium. Some glucosamine–chondroitin sulfate supplements contain these minerals, as well as other supporting substances. Do not give separate supplements of either mineral to your pet unless your veterinarian recommends it.

Manganese

This trace mineral, found in such common foods as egg yolks, nuts, seeds, whole-grain cereals, and leafy, green vegetables, reinforces the benefits of glucosamine and chondroitin sulfate by stimulating the production of cartilage. Manganese also functions as an antioxidant, slowing free-radical damage of joint tissues. In fact, a manganese deficiency can result in osteoarthritis. As noted above, this important mineral is added to some glucosamine-chondroitin

> **A protocol based on glucosamine and chondroitin sulfate supplementation may be enhanced with the addition of selenium, a frequently overlooked mineral.**

supplements, which is fortunate because processed foods intended for human consumption and most commercial pet foods usually do not contain manganese. As discussed in Chapter 4, manganese has been shown clinically to have a synergistic effect with glucosamine and chondroitin sulfate.

Selenium

This trace mineral is present in very small, but essential, quantities in both humans and animals. As mentioned earlier, selenium is an antioxidant and supports joint health by eliminating free radicals and bolstering the immune system. In humans, there is evidence that selenium preserves the elasticity of tissues by preventing oxidation of polyunsaturated fatty acids. Selenium works in tandem with another powerful antioxidant, vitamin E.

Selenium is found in whole grains and cereals. But when grains are refined, as much as 50 to 75 percent of the selenium can be lost. Selenium content is also reduced when food is heated or processed. Several foods that are often used as ingredients in pet foods — organ and muscle meats, cereals, whole wheat, and fish such as tuna, salmon, and shrimp — contain selenium. If dietary levels of selenium are inadequate, and your pet has osteoarthritis, consider adding a selenium supplement to your pet's diet if you are giving it glucosamine and chondroitin sulfate.

•   •   •

As you can see, the issue of vitamins and minerals for pets is just as complex and confusing as it is for humans. We genuinely wish there were a way to streamline it. But at this point the best we can do is inform you of the importance of vitamins and minerals, not only to your pet's overall health but especially when it comes to augmenting the glucosamine–chondroitin sulfate at the heart of the Arthritis Cure. By following these guidelines and your veterinarian's recommendations, you should be able to find a multi-purpose vitamin-mineral product that will boost the Arthritis Cure for Pets quickly and effectively.

Healthy Food, Healthy Pets

Imagine how simple life would be if we could eat anything we wanted and still thrive. Instead, eating has become a daily challenge for many people. Preparing appropriate meals for food sensitivities and allergies, special diets, and just plain old nutritious eating can be time consuming. But the fact of the matter is, the payoff is good health. Scientists now know that humans with arthritis can reduce many symptoms by eating properly. With a few modifications, that same good dietary advice can work for animals too.

As discussed in the previous chapter, certain vitamins and minerals prevent and slow the progress of osteoarthritis, and healthy fats reduce inflammation. So including those foods in an anti-arthritis diet plan makes sense. Raw, unprocessed foods may also promote joint health. Being overweight definitely makes the symptoms of arthritis worse, in man and beast, so it's important that the diet you choose for your pet is one that keeps the animal lean and fit.

Designing a Diet for Your Pet

Take extra care when purchasing pet foods. Quality ingredients pay off. Although many people balk at the price tags on the better pet foods, it is usually cheaper to buy the best than pay for treating an ailment caused by an inadequate diet. And your pet will be happier, too. Quality foods from such companies as Iams, Hills, Innovative Animal Diets, Purina, and Waltham are among the top choices. To understand why, let's take a look at the difference between quality pet food and other commercial varieties. By investigating various brands of pet food and becoming an informed consumer, you can make the best choice for your pet.

Commercial Pet Food

What you probably don't want to know about some brands of commercial pet foods: Much of the meat in canned food is made up of damaged and diseased parts of livestock and poultry. In fact, in all but two or three states it is legal to put meat from what is termed 4D sources in pet food. This is meat from animals that are dead, dying, disabled, or diseased upon their arrival at the slaughterhouse. Pet food is also allowed to contain food rejected by the FDA for human consumption, such as rancid animal fats and moldy grains. Meats and poultry in pet foods may also contain high levels of hormones, because these are routinely fed to livestock in the United States to encourage growth. Cats are particularly sensitive to these ingredients. Although there may be supervision of pet-food processing operations in some states, the FDA has no mandatory federal inspection of ingredients used in pet foods. Manufacturers are left free to use almost anything as ingredients. Fortunately, quality control has become a major issue with several of the top manufacturers of commercial pet foods, ensuring that your pet receives quality ingredients in an appropriately balanced proportion. Since a weakened immune system and osteoarthritis are often linked, it is important that a pet suffering from this disease be fed quality food. The questionable ingredients and contaminants in low-priced commercial foods simply cannot support the body functions of a healthy animal, let alone one with special nutritional needs.

> **If you are going to the special effort, and expense, of giving an arthritic pet supplements, then quality, nutritious food must be part of any treatment strategy.**

Carl learned this lesson the hard way when his twelve-year-old cat, Patsy, was diagnosed with osteoarthritis in her shoulder. The veterinarian recommended a glucosamine–chondroitin sulfate supplement. Being a devoted pet owner and confirmed cat person, Carl didn't hesitate to give Patsy the supplements. But he decided that, as a treat, he would let her eat as much tuna as she wanted, since it was her favorite food. At the volume-buying discount club Carl belonged to, he purchased a case of no-name kitty tuna, took it home, and let Patsy eat her fill. Before long she was vomiting and had developed diarrhea. To make matters worse, her arthritis was so bad that she was having trouble getting into the litter box.

At the veterinarian, Carl learned that he erred on the side of kindness, as well as thriftiness. By letting Patsy gorge on her favorite food, she had gained a pound, which stressed her sore shoulder joint even more. In addition, the low-quality food Carl had purchased had upset her stomach. That, in turn, had made it hard for her to absorb the nutrients in the arthritis supplements, so her shoulder joint became even more painful. When Carl left the veterinarian's, he took a case of top-quality cat food with him, as well as a newfound respect for the power of proper nutrition.

Additives to avoid: A close examination of the ingredients list on the package of pet food you normally buy is worth your time and effort. Ingredients are listed in order of quantity. (The same is true for human food. If your favorite brand of packaged cake has an ingredients list that starts with the word *sugar,* not *flour,* you can be sure it will be sweet!) Soft-moist burger products developed for dogs typically contain corn syrup as their third ingredient, and possibly sucrose as well. Both are sweeteners. Corn syrup is chemically derived from cornstarch, but in the body it generates the same peaks and valleys in blood glucose as common white sugar. As the body converts these sugars to energy, it uses up B vitamins and magnesium that are needed for joint health. Consuming large amounts of sugar can also make a pet obese. The body can store only a small amount of sugar at any one time. If an animal takes in a large quantity at one meal, which is possible with the sugar-added pet foods available today, the body converts the majority of the sugar to fat and stores it. Many of you may be aware that diabetes is a devastating problem that can result from humans on long-term diets containing excessive sugar.

A pet owner needs to read pet-food labels with an educated eye. Look for a product that lists a protein (such as meat) as the first ingredient. Keep in mind that sugar has many other names, including sucrose, dextrose, fructose, corn syrup, corn sweetener, malt syrup, and molasses. In cat food, the form of sugar listed is probably propylene glycol, which can make up as much as 10 percent of the calories. In dog food, sugars may constitute as much as 25 percent of a semi-moist dog food and a large percentage of dog biscuits as well.

What can be done about the shortcomings in commercial pet foods? Some animal owners have had great success with home-cooked meals. This is certainly one option, and it guarantees that your pet will receive optimal-quality ingredients. It is possible to buy organic meats of all kinds, free of hormones and antibiotics, and prepare them yourself for your pet's dinner. You can invent tasty combination dishes, working with grains, vegetables, nuts, seeds, fish, and meat, and prepare some in advance to freeze and defrost later. If your dog or cat is uncomfortable and needs aggressive treatment, home cooking can be very helpful. A month or two of custom feeding may give your pet a good start back on the road to health. (And who knows, after seeing the results, you may decide to feed yourself more selectively too.)

But since most people are too busy to feed themselves properly, let alone their pets, a good alternative is to purchase a top-quality pet food and give your pet additional fresh foods, including vegetables and meat.

Raw Foods

Whether you decide to prepare your pet's meals from scratch or work out some compromise plan, it is a good idea to include some raw foods each day. There's good reason for this. In their natural state, animals of course eat only a raw-foods diet. The advantage of such food is that it contains quantities of vitamins and minerals that help support strong immune function, important in managing osteoarthritis.

Just as important, raw foods are rich in living enzymes. These substances, which are destroyed by cooking, are important to digestion. The enzyme protease, for example, breaks down protein; amylase acts on starch; and lipase digests fats. These same substances also help prevent arthritis. As good nutrition supports joint health, enzymes help ensure that the joints receive adequate nourishment.

> **Raw foods contain living enzymes that play a role in preventing inflammation.**

Many people are not aware of the power of enzymes when it comes to health and well-being. Enzymes act as catalysts, triggering thousands of chemical reactions throughout the body. Without enzymes, the many tasks that cells must perform would not be possible. Consequently, malfunctions occur in tissues, organs, and, eventually, the whole body. Humans sometimes experience a lack of enzymes as chronic fatigue.

While cooking breaks down hard-to-digest fiber and muscle tissues, it also destroys a portion of the vitamins and minerals, as well as the enzymes. As a result, a diet of only cooked foods is not recommended, especially for pets with arthritis.

Studies on the Benefits of Raw Foods

In the 1930s Dr. Francis M. Pottenger compared the effects of cooked versus raw foods on the immune system of several generations of cats. This landmark work, now known as the Pottenger Cat Studies, grouped a number of cats into those that were given only raw food (specifically meat, bones, milk, and cod liver oil) and those that were given the same foods, but either partially or fully cooked. Dr. Pottenger found that all the cats in the group consuming only raw foods were completely healthy and never needed treatment by a veterinarian. In the population of cats eating cooked food, however, the more cooked the food was, the less healthy the cats became. Irritable bowel syndrome, hepatitis, heart lesions, feline urologic syndrome, and arthritis were only a few of the debilitating diseases these cats developed. When they were given a raw-foods diet, though, their immune systems improved. But even so, their damaged immune systems were passed on to the next generation. These third-generation off-spring were fed raw foods, but it took another generation for immune-system functions to be restored fully.

This type of immune-system deterioration occurs because certain essential nutrients are lacking in cooked food. Subsequent research has shown that the amino acid taurine is an absolute necessity for good health in cats. Humans can manufacture taurine, but cats cannot. In nature they obtain it from their diet of raw foods. But a house cat may have a hard time getting enough taurine. Although it is added to cat foods and supplements, pet owners who give their cats meat cooked at home are feeding them a taurine-poor diet. Roasted meat has lost 52 percent of its taurine, and boiling removes 79 percent.

If Pottenger's study is not impressive enough, there is a report about raw foods that is hard to forget. In India a physician named Sir Robert McCarrison tested the same notion some years ago. The doctor fed one thousand laboratory rats a variety of fresh foods, including raw carrots, cabbage, sprouted beans, raw whole milk, whole-wheat flatbread, and once a week a small amount of meat and bones.

After twenty-seven months — the equivalent of 55 human years — the rats were autopsied. Dr. McCarrison found no signs of disease at all. He then experimented with two other diets, one consisting of foods eaten by poor people in India, and the other composed of foods eaten by the English poor. Rats eating the Indian diet developed diseases in every organ, while the rats on the English fare of boiled, sweetened, and canned foods became so hyperactive that they literally ate one another, with the weaker rats being consumed first. Studies like Pottenger's and McCarrison's certainly drive home the point that raw foods are critical for the health of all animals, including your pet.

Seasonings

Whether you choose to make your own pet food or purchase a good commercial brand, you may find that your companion animal enjoys a little extra flavor added to its daily meal. For best results, try one condiment or spice at a time, use it for a few days, and then rotate to another. That certain herbs and spices are antiarthritic is anecdotal, not based on research studies.

Garlic

Add a freshly grated garlic clove, or a portion of one, to a pet's food. Or the garlic can be chopped and placed in a pint jar of apple cider vinegar or brown rice vinegar. These are preferable to white vinegar, which has been heated or distilled. Close the lid on the jar tightly and allow it to stand for a few weeks. You'll have a garlic tincture that can be added to foods in small amounts (⅛ teaspoon for a cat or small dog, ½ teaspoon for a medium dog, 1 teaspoon for a large dog).

Turmeric

This ancient spice has long been used to reduce swelling and lessen inflammation caused by wounds, bruises, and insect bites. An animal patient with osteoarthritis may benefit from this peppery flavoring, although its "bite" could be a bit strong for some animals. Turmeric purportedly enhances immunity and counteracts toxins. It may also function as a natural cortisone, stimulating the adrenals to release compounds called corticosteroids. Turmeric has no known side effects. And again, no research has substantiated any of these claims.

Ginger

You can try adding a bit of minced fresh ginger to your pet's next meal, but, again, it may be a bit too strong for some animals' taste.

Special Nutrients for Osteoarthritis

B Vitamins

Studies show that vitamin B_6 is essential to joint health. Various research projects have demonstrated that a deficiency of vitamin B_6, also known as pyridoxine, is associated with degeneration of joint tissues. In one such clinical trial, for example, fifteen chicks were raised on a normal diet for the first two weeks after hatching. Then they were switched to a diet lacking vitamin B_6 for six weeks.

> **Meat is a good source of vitamin B_6.**

When the chicks were examined, researchers found swollen ankle joints and abnormal gait. Close inspection of their joint cartilage revealed fissures, as well as evidence that glycosaminoglycans (GAGs) had migrated from the knee cartilage surface into the synovial fluid.[51]

Similar results were obtained in a second study, when researchers found that a deficiency of vitamin B_6 in birds caused proteoglycans, which are normally bound to joint cartilage, to escape into the synovial fluid.[52]

In addition to their abilities to strengthen joints, the B vitamins perform one other particularly useful task — they detoxify the body from the additives in the pet foods, like preservatives, artificial coloring, and hormones. The B-complex of vitamins also support the liver as they break down toxins and deactivate hormones so they can be excreted.

Furthermore, there is evidence that both B_{12} and folic acid lessen the pain associated with osteoarthritis. Why this occurs is not clear. It may be that these B vitamins, or the entire B complex, facilitate enzymes in triggering chemical reactions. This, in turn, could slow cartilage tissue degeneration, enhance its functions, and, as a result, decrease pain.

Flavonoids

We already know that flavonoids can help osteoarthritis. Besides functioning as plant pigments, flavonoids support vitamin C in promoting joint health, help strengthen the structure of collagen, and provide both antioxidants and anti-inflammatory functions.

Flavonoids' usefulness in treating osteoarthritis was established in a study of thirty patients with knee osteoarthritis. In those treated with flavonoids, the authors found a "marked curative effect."[53]

Healthy Oils That Lessen Inflammation

As discussed in the previous chapter, although fats have a reputation for being unhealthy, certain oils — known as essential fatty acids (EFAs) — can actually help the arthritic patient, both human and animal. First, a brief background on various oils.

Oils are fats that are liquid at room temperature. Some oils are categorized as omega-6 fatty acids, and others are known as omega-3s. These fatty acids are the raw material that make up prostaglandins, hormonelike molecules that can trigger inflammation in a variety of body tissues.

The important thing to remember is that omega-6 fatty acids have a tendency to convert to the inflammatory prostaglandins, while the omega-3 fatty acids convert to the noninflammatory prostaglandins. And where are these omega-3 fatty acids found in the food supply? In fish oils, walnuts, and flaxseed as well as flaxseed oil. They are also available commercially, as a supplement.

> An easy way to quell inflammation in your house pets is to add some flaxseed oil to your dog's food and to prepare a fish dinner for your cat! Cold-water fish, such as salmon and tuna, are an excellent source. Canola oil is another option.

As the omega-6 fatty acids convert to prostaglandins, arachidonic acid forms. Arachidonic acid eventually turns into the type of prostaglandins that can worsen the symptoms of osteoarthritis. Unfortunately, arachidonic acid is also plentiful in beef, pork, lamb, turkey, and chicken. In addition, organ meats commonly used in pet foods, such as heart and kidney, have high levels of arachidonic acid.

The conscientious pet owner is now presented with a true quandary. How can you feed your pet the meat it needs to be healthy without making the symptoms of arthritis worse? Actually, this is where the omega-3s come to the rescue. You can counteract the effects of arachidonic acid by adding omega-3-rich flaxseed or flaxseed oil to a diet of whole grains, vegetables, and moderate amounts of fish and chicken. The omega-3s in the flaxseed can then reduce any inflammation caused by the arachidonic acid. Find out from your veterinarian what is the most appropriate level of flaxseed or flaxseed oil to add to your pet's diet.

Osteoarthritis and Excess Weight

Any regimen designed to prevent or slow the course of degenerative joint disease should include weight control. Excess weight can increase symptoms of the disease simply by putting more stress on joints. Furthermore, it prevents an animal from moving freely. An overweight cat, for example, cannot move with the supple grace nature intended, and its limited range of motion can lead to other physical problems. If the cat also has arthritis, being overweight only increases the lack of mobility.

According to a study published in 1997 in *Veterinary Clinics of North America,* there are no precise figures on the frequency of obesity in dogs and cats. But preliminary figures from a national epidemiological study reveal that about 25 percent of dogs and cats are either overweight or actually obese. (In this instance, obesity is defined as a state in which an animal has gained sufficient weight to impair its health and normal ability to function. Or an animal may be diagnosed as obese when its weight exceeds 20 percent of its ideal body weight for breed and gender.)[54]

In animal medicine today, obesity is often overlooked as a contributing factor to disease, particularly when an animal is in the early stages of an ailment and significant symptoms have not yet developed. Although in the past there was a lack of research focusing on the relationship of obesity to arthritis in household pets, information has been culled from studies with different species to show an association between obesity and musculoskeletal problems. We anxiously await the results of several studies currently under way to evaluate the effects of obesity on pets with osteoarthritis. In human studies, excess weight has been identified as a risk factor for osteoarthritis, particularly in the knee. Added weight could damage cartilage, or metabolic imbalances caused by the weight may change the cellular environment of the joint and chemically alter joint tissue.

A study conducted by researchers at Ralston Purina investigated the relationship between the quantity of food an animal consumes and the frequency and severity of osteoarthritis. The researchers divided eight-week-old Labrador retrievers into two groups of forty-eight. The animals were then paired according to gender and body weight. All the dogs received the same diet. But within each pair, one dog was fed with no limit (ad libitum) and the other was limit-fed, so that it received 75 percent of the amount eaten the previous day by its ad libitum–fed partner.

At various ages — four months, six months, and one, two, three, and five years of age — the dogs were evaluated for bone health, including frequency and severity of osteoarthritis. Using X rays of hip (coxofemoral) joints, researchers found that the Labradors that were allowed to eat freely had a greater frequency of — as well as more severe — osteoarthritis. They concluded that limiting the amount a dog eats can effectively minimize the development of this disease in these joints.[55] Other studies have also shown that weight loss resulted in improvements in dogs with hip dysplasia.

Not all studies support the theory that excess weight is associated with a higher risk of osteoarthritis, however. One clinical trial involving monkeys determined that there was no correlation between joint cartilage deterioration and weight. It may be that certain species react differently to obesity. Or perhaps it was because monkeys walk on all fours, distributing their weight over more joints, instead of just legs, hips, knees, and feet. Until more research is done, though, it would be wise to keep your pet as trim as possible. Besides osteoarthritis, obesity is associated with a host of other health problems in humans and animals.[56]

The same weight-loss rule that applies to humans is also true for animals — less food, more exercise. The amount of food an overweight animal gets each day can be reduced by 30 to 40 percent until the desired weight is reached. Don't forget to eliminate snacks high in calories or fat. If you can't resist giving a snack because of that sad, dramatically pathetic look your pet gives you, try giving raw fruits or vegetables instead. Many dogs love the taste of carrots, green beans, and other vegetables. Combining this approach with an exercise program can produce results faster, as well as improve symptoms of osteoarthritis (more on this in the following chapter). For a pet, losing 1 to 2 percent of body weight per week is a healthy weight-loss goal.

At first, you may want to reduce your pet's meals by less than the suggested 30 to 40 percent. Studies have shown that drastic decreases in calories for humans can backfire. You may recall the sensation "set-point" theory caused when it was discovered a few years ago. According to this school of thought, if you deprive your body of calories, it believes a famine is occurring. Nature's way of protecting us against this dangerous situation is still with us today, even though famines are not (at least, not in industrialized nations). So when calories are cut, nature comes to our rescue by slowing the metabolism and reducing the number of calories that are burned. Some weight loss may take place, but when normal eating resumes, calories are even harder to burn off with the new, lower metabolism. The body stores the unused calories as fat, in case the "famine" returns.

One way to avoid this possibility is to start your pet's diet with moderate calorie restriction, and decrease the amount of food further if you don't see results within a few weeks.

Tips for Putting Your Pet on a Diet

- Feed your pet three small meals a day, and do not leave out any food between mealtimes.
- Remember, slow weight loss is more successful than rapid weight loss, over the long term. Don't rush the diet.
- Give your pet structured exercise.
- Consider filling, high-fiber food to dampen appetite. Add oat or wheat bran, plus plenty of cooked vegetables (carrots, peas, baked potatoes) to your pet's diet.
- Avoid giving your pet a diet rich in organ meats like liver. These are naturally high in saturated fats. There are also high-fiber kibbles that you can purchase from your veterinarian or at your local pet store.
- Check your pet's coat for oiliness. An oily coat is a sign of an overly fatty diet. Oily wastes are discharged through the skin's pores. An all-meat diet may be responsible. If so, look for foods with varied ingredients, like whole grains and vegetables.
- Read pet-food labels, keeping an eye out for added sugar and salt, both of which can promote weight gain.
- Train yourself to say no to food when your pet begs for more food, and yes to hugs.
- Last but not least, do not feed your pet bits of food when you are eating. These small "snacks" can add up quickly when it comes to calories.

Salt and Weight Loss

Salt, also known as sodium chloride, attracts water. A diet high in salt can cause the body to retain water, resulting in a form of weight gain. Popular weight-loss diets often take advantage of this phenomenon and promote rapid weight loss in the first few days while fluids are being excreted. The salt content of a pet's diet should be considered in any weight-loss plan.

•   •   •

In rare cases, there may be a disease at the root of a pet's weight problem. If your pet does not lose weight after a month of restricted calories and exercise, check with a veterinarian. Your dog or cat may be suffering from hyperthyroidism or hyper-adrenocorticism.

Modifying Your Own Behavior

For humans, food and love are intertwined. But the epidemic of obesity in the Western world has created something of a love-hate relationship as well. Although dieting is a national obsession, most pet owners overfeed their beloved animals, in the "food is love" spirit. Food is often left out, available at all hours of the day. With so many commercial pet foods low in nutrients, animals continue to eat, searching for the much-needed nutrients that are in short supply. In addition, poor-quality pet foods provide more than enough protein, which is metabolized and stored as fat. These foods also have a high percentage of calories from fats and sugar, as well as excess salt. All these factors contribute to obesity in animals. But remember, these are factors you can control. By changing your pet's diet to healthier fare, you can delay — and possibly even avoid — the onset of osteoarthritis in a younger animal and alleviate many symptoms in a pet that already has the disease. All in all, providing your pet with a nutritious diet can go a long way toward making it healthier and happier.

CHAPTER
8

Other Treatments for Arthritis: What Works and What Doesn't

Traditionally, one of the most difficult aspects of dealing with arthritis has been its being thought of as a chronic condition, meaning it does not go away. In fact, typically the situation continued to deteriorate until movement was severely restricted. Until recently an arthritis sufferer — whether human or animal — had few options other than pain relievers, which, as we have seen, do not treat the disease itself, only the symptoms.

With the advent of glucosamine and chondroitin sulfate, physicians, veterinarians, and patients have discovered a highly effective method of dealing with osteoarthritis. In addition, there are many other therapies, including acupuncture, massage, hydrotherapy, and herbs, that work quite well as enhancers for this treatment. With only slight modification, most of these adjunctive therapies work as well on animals as on humans. In fact, the tremendous popularity of alternative health remedies for humans has led many pet owners to seek out similar medications and techniques to treat animal ailments. It should be emphasized that these alternative therapies should be considered a complement to the Arthritis Cure for Pets, *not* a primary treatment. Pets suffering from osteoarthritis should be treated with glucosamine and chondroitin sulfate, painkillers when needed, proper diet, and controlled exercise. See Chapter 5 for the complete Six-Step Arthritis Cure for Pets Program.

Some of these approaches, like acupuncture, are now accepted by mainstream medicine. Others are supported only by anecdotal evidence. An overview of some alternative methods for coping with osteoarthritis in your pet is presented below. You may find that one — or more — of them is ideal for complementing the Arthritis Cure for Pets. Keep in mind, however, that much of the information in this chapter is based on common practice or anecdotal evidence. There is still very little research on herbs and other therapies when used for animals — unlike the Arthritis Cure for Pets.

Acupuncture Points to Relief

Acupuncture, a form of traditional Chinese medicine that involves placing slender needles in certain points on the body, made headlines not long ago when it became one of the first so-called alternative health treatments to be recognized by major health-insurance companies. In legitimizing acupuncture, Western medical authorities have at long last put their stamp of approval on a practice that is thousands of years old. In fact, acupuncture was used on animals as far back as three thousand years ago, according to documents in India that describe ailing elephants being treated with needles.

In this country animal acupuncture began gaining popularity about thirty years ago. And since 1997, when the National Institutes of Health published its groundbreaking report on the effectiveness of acupuncture in treating certain types of pain, it has become a fairly common treatment, especially for arthritis.

Although acupuncture was once considered something of a mystery, which may explain why it took so long for it to be accepted by mainstream medicine, today scientists know that it works by releasing the brain's own natural painkillers, known as endorphins, into the body. In other words, it accomplishes the same thing as giving your pet a pharmaceutical painkiller, but without the side effects or the unpleasantness of forcing your pet to swallow a pill.

There are two theories — Chinese and Western — about how acupuncture should be done. A tenet of traditional Chinese medicine is that the life force known as chi can become blocked, causing a variety of ailments. Acupuncture releases the chi so that energy can flow throughout the body once again. But to work, traditional acupuncture must be performed by someone trained in the procedure. There are almost 700 possible insertion points (known as acupoints) in the human body and 112 in dogs, and often the acupoint is nowhere near the actual pain.

In the Westernized version of acupuncture, needles are placed near the painful area. It is still important to have a qualified acupuncturist perform the treatment, however. There have been reports of severe injuries caused by inexperienced people attempting to "do it yourself."

The course of treatment with acupuncture usually involves one roughly thirty-minute session a week for about one month. If there is no improvement in the pet's condition after four treatments, it's unlikely that additional treatments will produce results, and the acupuncture is usually discontinued.

Although people often wince at the thought of needles piercing their skin, animals don't have the same fears, and the procedure is virtually painless. With animals, the most difficult aspect of acupuncture can be simply getting them to lie still. Calm pets generally do better than more high-strung ones and may even doze off while they wait for the treatment to be completed.

If you are interested in pursuing acupuncture for your pet, ask your veterinarian for a recommendation or contact the International Veterinary Acupuncture Society for a referral (see the sidebar at the end of this chapter).

Acupressure

Acupressure is a good alternative to acupuncture, especially for pet owners. Acupressure is based on the same theory, but instead of needles it involves pressure from the fingers at specific points on the body. With a little training from a licensed therapist, a pet owner can perform acupressure at home, and since it is noninvasive, there is no danger of harming your pet. It can be used in conjunction with acupuncture or as a substitute.

Chiropractic Care

Practiced for more than a hundred years on humans, chiropractic — and its close relative, osteopathy — is used on animals these days. It is especially helpful for acute pain, such as sore joints. It is ideal for show and racehorses, as well as racing, hunting, or agility-training dogs, since these animals can injure or strain themselves. Helping the joint tissues heal properly, say the experts, makes the horse or dog less likely to develop arthritis at an early age. Chiropractic is also used frequently with dogs such as corgis and dachshunds, whose short legs and long backs can create back problems at an early age. Although cats aren't as likely to suffer from these types of joint problems, they can strain muscles and have also been known to benefit from chiropractic.

The theory behind chiropractic, as well as other manipulative therapies, centers on the belief that the spine must be in proper alignment for the body to function properly. Poor spinal alignment, or subluxation, can be the result of injury, genetics, posture, stress, and other factors. When subluxation occurs, the energy from nerves that pass through the spinal column is blocked. Disease, pain, and other unhealthful conditions are the result of the blockage, but the situation can be corrected by manipulating various parts of the body with the hands.

In years past, chiropractic was considered to be a "fringe" treatment, if not outright quackery. Today studies have repeatedly shown that it is not only safe but effective in treating back problems in humans. And in 1996 the American Veterinary Medical Association reviewed the available animal studies and concluded that "evidence exists to indicate that veterinary chiropractic can be beneficial."

Anecdotal evidence of chiropractic's success with animals is abundant. Dogs, cats, and horses have all benefited from this relatively painless, inexpensive treatment for acute conditions. So although there are no long-term studies showing the effects of chiropractic on chronic osteoarthritis, pet owners may want to try it along with the Arthritis Cure for Pets.

Correctly performing chiropractic on animals involves a thorough understanding of their anatomy. In other words, even though you may have had chiropractic yourself, *do not* try it at home on your pet. To find a qualified animal chiropractor, ask your veterinarian for a referral.

Although manual manipulation of the spine is the traditional method of chiropractic, a new variation involving an instrument known as an activator machine was introduced a few years ago. Borrowed from human chiropractic, the activator is a metal, plungerlike device that the veterinarian pops above each vertebra. The gentle force of the popping plunger realigns any vertebrae that are out of place.

The activator method was introduced into veterinary practice after Dr. William Inman, a Washington veterinarian, had a chiropractor friend try it as a last-ditch effort on a dachshund that was immobilized from the neck down because of back problems. The dachshund walked out of the vet's office, and Inman now instructs other veterinarians in the use of the activator. Some of these doctors report a success rate as high as 85 percent on patients with osteoarthritis.

Herbal Remedies

Herbs were the first medicines humans used to cure their aches, pains, and other ailments. And, of course, wild animals often rely on locally available plants when they feel ill, just as our own dogs and cats seek out grass for an upset stomach.

Herbal remedies are undergoing a major revival. Medicines in this category that are in common use today have stood the test of time. After centuries of use, most have proved safe for humans, but by and large, their effect on animals is not known. Keep in mind that herbal medicine is a discipline of its own and requires expert advice. Before beginning any herbal remedies, consult your veterinarian or an alternative-medicine practitioner who specializes in pets.

Boswellia

Boswellia, or *Boswellia serrata* as it is called botanically, is actually the gummy resin of a large branching tree native to India. Although no one knows exactly how it works, it has long been used there as a medicine and is used for the treatment of osteoarthritis as well as forms of rheumatoid arthritis, fibromyalgia, and lower back pain.

> Herbs that have been proposed for use in the treatment of arthritis in animals include boswellia, devil's claw root, feverfew, and yucca. Others, such as dandelion and nettle, have been touted as having more general healing powers. Unfortunately, their side effects or effectiveness in treating arthritis is unknown. No controlled, randomized studies have been performed to evaluate them.

In the United States anecdotal evidence of Boswellia's success in treating the painful symptoms of arthritis in cats, dogs, and horses has been reported. Dogs with hip dysplasia and spinal arthritis, as well as horses with chronic arthritis and a variety of skeletal injuries, have reportedly been helped by Boswellia.

Boswellia is available in powder and capsule form. There are also Boswellia creams that can be applied externally on the affected area; the active ingredients are absorbed into the system through the skin.

> It should be noted that Boswellia is effective only when in use and does not halt or prevent arthritis. If supplementation is stopped, symptoms return.

Devil's Claw Root

Devil's claw root, known botanically as *Harpagophytum procumbens,* is native to southern Africa. Its unusual name was inspired by the plant's striking fruit, which has small hooks protruding from its skin. The active component in devil's claw root is harpagoside. This compound was tested in pharmacological screening trials, and its anti-inflammatory abilities were confirmed. Studies abroad in the 1950s showed the root to be effective at reducing the inflammation and swelling caused by experimentally induced arthritis. However, later research did not support those findings.[57]

Today devil's claw root is a popular treatment for arthritis in Europe. Still, not all human arthritis patients find devil's claw root effective. And its effectiveness in treating arthritis in dogs and horses has not been studied. Since it is known to increase the production of stomach acid, it could cause an upset stomach and is not recommended for a pet that is taking painkillers.

Yucca

Yucca (*Yucca schidigera* and other species) is native to the deserts of the southwestern United States. The fruit is considered a delicacy and is the ingredient that causes root beer to foam, but yucca also contains saponin, a therapeutic compound that studies have shown to be 60 percent effective in reducing human arthritic symptoms such as swelling, pain, and stiffness. In light of this research, it is now being considered as a treatment for arthritis in animals. It has no known toxicity. No controlled studies have been performed to date that would demonstrate its effectiveness for treating arthritis in animals.

Nettle

Another herb that can come to the aid of an arthritic pet is stinging nettle (*Urtica dioica*), which takes its name from the bristly hairs covering its surface. Although nettle is an unpleasant plant to have around — the bristly hairs can puncture the skin like miniature needles and cause an itching rash or tiny blisters — as a supplement, it is a powerhouse. Nettle is packed with nutrients, including vitamin A, beta-carotene, B-complex, vitamin C, and vitamin D, along with the minerals magnesium, calcium, phosphorus, potassium, and iron. It is considered an antispasmodic, which helps relax muscles, and has a long history of use in human medicine. It is still prescribed for arthritis in people. Using nettle for arthritis in animals has been suggested, but there are no studies evaluating its effectiveness. Nettle can be given to a pet in capsule form or as a tincture. There have been rare reports of allergic reaction to nettle.

Horsetail

Horsetail (*Equisetum arvense*) has been proved clinically to help mend connective tissue and bone by stimulating the metabolic repair processes. Although no one knows exactly how it works, horsetail may replace lost silicon, one of the minerals that make up the complex structure of healthy bone.[58] Body stores of silicon decline with age.

In humans, horsetail has a special affinity for the nails and hair and may function in the same way in animals, improving the coat, skin, and claws from the inside out, although this has not been shown clinically.

How Homeopathy Helps

Homeopathy is best explained with the phrase "like cures like." The Greek physician Hippocrates, considered to be the father of medicine, believed in this principle, as have many other healers. A homeopathic treatment for hives, for example, would be a highly diluted solution of a substance that would normally produce hivelike symptoms in a healthy person. According to the Law of Similars, these minute doses activate the body's own healing process and enable it to conquer the illness. Since homeopathic remedies are so highly diluted, there are seldom any toxic effects. However, these medicines can be dangerous, even lethal, if they are not prepared by experienced practitioners. Considering that there are a mind-boggling 2,500 homeopathic remedies available, it is easy to see why this field is not for novices. The American Holistic Veterinary Medical Association can provide you with a list of homeopathic veterinarians (see sidebar at the end of this chapter).

Although homeopathic remedies are widely studied in humans, and the majority of studies support their effectiveness, there is no similar body of research with animals. There are, however, many anecdotal tales of these medicines working virtual miracles with pets. Homeopathy is relatively inexpensive and safe, so it may be worth investigating.

Hydrotherapy and Healing

If you have ever soothed sore muscles in a whirlpool bath, you have firsthand experience with the benefits of hydrotherapy. For centuries man and beast alike have sought out hot springs and warm mineral waters all around the world. Today practitioners of hydrotherapy have turned what some people still think of as an indulgence into a science.

Hydrotherapy utilizes water of all temperatures, hot compresses, and ice packs to treat a variety of conditions. Warm water, for example, enlarges the blood vessels, which in turn supplies more blood to the muscles and skin, a process that allows stiff limbs and joints to relax. Cold water does just the opposite, slowing blood flow and reducing inflammation. Swimming can also be used as therapy. Because the body weight is supported by water, the sore limb or joint can be strengthened through exercise without further aggravating the problem.

Hydrotherapists outfit an animal with a special "lifejacket" and leash, so there is no danger of drowning. The most difficult thing about hydrotherapy is finding a place to practice it. There are specialized facilities for exercising injured dogs and horses, but they are few and far between. And many pet owners who have swimming pools, whirlpools, and hot tubs are hesitant about putting their pet in the water — with good reason. Whirl-pools and hot tubs are especially dangerous. Dogs can overheat easily and should not be allowed to spend more than a few super-vised moments in either one. As for swimming pools, letting a dog swim with its owner may result in the dog jumping in the pool when it is alone and not being able to find its way out. By the way, although hydrotherapy is safe and effective, it is not rec-ommended for dogs that do not like water, since the experience will be too stressful. And as most cat owners can attest, our feline friends are not good prospects for hydrotherapy.

A variation known as isokinetic relaxation is also available in a few areas. This form of hydrotherapy consists of simultaneous movement, retraining, and relaxation of the muscles. Three 45- to 60-minute sessions on three consecutive days are required to initiate the treatment. At the end of the third session, symptoms in approximately 80 to 90 percent of the dogs are significantly improved. Arthritis, hip and elbow dysplasia, performance in agility/obedience trials, pre- and postsurgical conditioning, and even paralysis can be treated with isokinetic relaxation. The supplements used in the Arthritis Cure for Pets are recommended in conjunction with this form of therapy. According to anecdotal evidence, the treatment is remarkably successful. One West Coast facility that offers isokinetic relaxation is Almaden Valley Animal Hospital, 15790 Almaden Expressway, San Jose, CA 95120; 408-997-0828; http://www.dogtherapy.com.

Magnet Magic

Magnets have been used to ease pain for thousands of years. In ancient Egypt, Greece, and China, magnets were used to treat a variety of ailments, including arthritis. In this country magnet therapy continued until the late 1800s, when unscrupulous "healers" made exaggerated claims. Eventually they were dismissed as quacks and drummed out of business. Not surprisingly, the popularity of magnets disappeared with them.

Today, though, backed by dozens of studies worldwide, magnets are gaining acceptance once again. Germany, Japan, Russia, Israel, and forty-five other countries consider magnets a legitimate medical treatment for everything from broken bones to anxiety and depression. As sports fans know, a significant number of golfers on the professional circuit swear by magnets, and baseball players are often seen wearing them in one form or another. In the animal world, horse owners frequently use magnets with great success. Now, more small-animal owners are discovering the benefits too.

The type of magnets used to treat pain are not the same as the ones holding notes on the refrigerator door. While the common household magnet usually measures about 200 gauss (the term for measuring strength of a magnetic field), therapeutic, or permanent, magnets are more likely to be in the 2,500 gauss range.

(Electromagnetism, which involves electrical pulsing, is another effective means of using magnets to heal, but it is not something that can be done at home. When we speak of magnets, we are referring only to the permanent variety.)

Although no one knows exactly how magnets work therapeutically, there is no doubt that they do. In Tokyo a 1996 study comparing the effects of acupuncture and magnets on painful muscles found that magnets worked just as well as acupuncture.[59]

In the United States magnets have proved effective at relieving the pain of postpolio syndrome. In a study of fifty people debilitated with this painful condition, twenty-two of the twenty-nine fitted with magnets reported to researchers that they experienced a 50 percent reduction in pain. The astonishing fact is that this relief came after forty-five minutes of wearing the magnet.[60]

A study conducted in Israel examined the effects of magnets on rats with artificially induced inflammation of the knee, a condition very similar to arthritis. Researchers found that inflammation decreased dramatically in eight out of ten rats in the test group, after exposure to a 3,800 gauss magnet. In the control group, however, no magnets were used and inflammation was twice as high as the test group.[61]

In addition to being effective, magnets have other benefits. First, they are safe and side effect–free. Second, they are relatively inexpensive. Third, they come in a variety of shapes, sizes, and styles and are even incorporated into things like mattress pads and pet beds.

For Maril, these advantages turned out to be a godsend when Chucky, her twelve-year-old Labrador mix, was diagnosed with arthritis. As their long hikes into the nearby mountains grew shorter, she searched with increasing desperation for something that would alleviate the stiffness in Chucky's rear legs. Then she remembered that a friend with joint problems had had great success with magnets. The friend put Maril in touch with a magnet company, and two days later Chucky was sleeping on a pet bed embedded with small magnets. To the delight of both Maril and Chucky, after about a week, he was noticeably better. And by month's end they were heading into the hills once again.

•   •   •

Magnets can be purchased at alternative health stores, on the Internet, and by mail order. Large companies that deal only in magnets, such as Nikken, offer catalogs with a wide range of products designed specifically for pets. Prices vary. Before investing in a large pet bed, which sells for about $150, you might want to try a simpler, less expensive approach, like a strap with magnets and a Velcro closure that can be placed almost anywhere on a pet's body. It is also possible to purchase individual magnets in various sizes that can be held in place with an elastic bandage. If that produces the desired results, then you can consider more expensive options.

Magnets are most effective when they are placed directly on the sore joint. Some practitioners believe they should be placed according to the principles of acupressure and acupuncture, and applied to alternate pressure points in the body. While studies have shown this method to reduce pain in both animals and humans, direct application is simpler and effective too. One reason magnet beds are popular for animals, though, is that they are so simple to use, especially for pets that balk at wearing things like elastic bandages.

Although magnets can alleviate the pain of osteoarthritis in some animals, they are not a cure and should be used as a *complement* to the Arthritis Cure for Pets, not in place of it.

Cartilage Extracts

Cartilage-extract supplements have proved effective in some cases of animal arthritis, but this approach remains controversial. Shark cartilage is a popular treatment for arthritis in horses and dogs. However, since there is no clinical research supporting the use of shark cartilage, a purified source of glycosaminoglycans would be a more clinically reliable option. Collagen compounds derived from cattle and chicken have also been used. Human studies with cartilage supplements suggest that these measures might be effective in reversing arthritis in people as well as in animals. A ninety-day study involving cartilage powder was conducted as a combined effort between the Boston Veterans Administration Hospital and Harvard Medical School. Researchers worked with twenty-nine patients with arthritis who were scheduled for joint-replacement surgery. Each morning the volunteers consumed one heaping teaspoonful of ground, dried chicken cartilage in their orange juice. Within the first ten days the participants reported that inflammation and pain had ceased. After thirty days mobility in the volunteers' joints increased. And at the end of the trial, full function was restored.

No comparable animal study exists, but there are ample reports from pet owners and veterinarians who have successfully used cartilage therapy on animals. Supplements are available as powders and extracts, derived from shark, poultry, or cow cartilage. These products contain a mixture of GAGs (glycosamino-glycans, the special proteins that bind water into the cartilage matrix). When looking for supplements, choose a purified source of GAGs, as contained, for example, in Cosequin.

Good Fats for Bad Joints: The Essential Fatty Acids

During the past few years we have repeatedly been told that fat is the enemy. Now researchers know this statement is only partially true. While saturated fats and trans fats are the ones to avoid, a whole other category known as essential fatty acids (EFA) are now in the spotlight. Found primarily in plant foods, cold-water fish, and herbs, EFAs are absolutely essential to good health (hence their name). There are two categories of EFAs — omega-3 and omega-6. Both are involved in creating prostaglandins, hormonelike substances that regulate the cardiovascular, reproductive, immune, and nervous systems. They provide protection for our bodies' cells by deciding what goes in and what comes out of each one. And they also produce anti-inflammatory prostaglandins, thereby making them useful for treating arthritis. In fact, research has shown that when animals consume foods high in EFAs, especially the omega-3s, changes occur in their cell walls that reduce the likelihood of inflammation. If your pet likes fish such as tuna, sardines, salmon, mackerel, herring, or cod, you're in luck. Three servings of these cold-water fish per week supply healthy amounts of omega-3s. They are also available in supplement form from pet stores and veterinarians. Derm Caps are one of the best-known, but there are others on the market.

Massage Makes a Difference

In almost all cultures worldwide, massage has been a respected therapeutic treatment for centuries. Like hydrotherapy, some people consider it an indulgence, but the fact of the matter is that studies have proved massage's ability to reduce pain, improve flexibility, and stimulate circulation of lymph and blood systems.

Massage accomplishes its good deeds in several ways. First, it stimulates the release of cytokines, natural substances that lower the levels of immune-system-destroying stress hormones. It also boosts circulation, providing extra oxygen to all areas of the body. In addition, it may encourage the brain to produce natural pain relievers known as endorphins.

One of the best things about massage, though, is that you can perform it on your pet yourself — and you both benefit! Your pet will be more relaxed, as well as enjoy the advantages mentioned above. Several studies have shown that the person giving the massage experiences lower blood pressure and heart rate, which means that you will be improving your health too.

There are many different kinds of massage, but for our purposes two types, known as effleurage and petrissage, are most useful. Effleurage involves slow, gentle stroking in only one direction. This procedure relaxes the pet and puts both of you at ease. On the other hand, the gentle kneading, pushing, and pulling of skin known as petrissage is more stimulating. A typical massage might begin with effleurage, move on to petrissage, then some easy stretching and flexing of the limbs, followed by more effleurage for a nice, relaxing conclusion. Massage sessions can be done in a few minutes (if you are on a tight schedule) or for longer periods of time. Some pet owners recommend massaging animals while you're sitting on the floor and watching television.

Beware of massaging the neck or back area if your pet has an injury there, and avoid any infected, bruised, or inflamed areas. If you feel uncomfortable massaging your pet or are worried about hurting it, there are a number of excellent books on massage, and your veterinarian may be able to recommend a professional therapist who is knowledgeable about pets. If so, he or she can demonstrate some basic massage techniques so that you can get a better idea of how to proceed on your own.

How to Contact Professional Alternative Health Organizations

Academy of Veterinary Homeopathy, 1283 Lincoln St., Eugene, OR 97401; (503) 342-7665

American Holistic Veterinary Medical Association, 2214 Old Emmorton Rd., Bel Air, MD 21014; (410) 569-0795

American Veterinary Chiropractic Association, P.O. Box 249, Port Byron, IL 61275; (309) 523-3995

International Veterinary Acupuncture Society, 2140 Conestoga Rd., Chester Springs, PA 19425; (610) 827-7245

CHAPTER
9

The Value of Exercise in Treating Arthritis

Exercise is not only essential for keeping any animal in good health, but it can also help reverse the effects of osteoarthritis in pets. While a healthy diet and glucosamine and chondroitin sulfate supplements can go a long way toward treating this disease, you can extend those benefits even further by making sure your pet gets adequate and appropriate exercise.

The Role of Exercise in a Complete Regimen for Healing Osteoarthritis

Like most rehabilitative programs, the Arthritis Cure for Pets is a combination approach that includes exercise as part of the therapy to get your pet up and moving again. Countless medical studies and clinical experiences underscore the importance of exercise in recovering from osteoarthritis. In fact, several recent studies confirm that treating osteoarthritis involves a three-step approach, consisting of moderate exercise, weight control, and use of anti-inflammatory medications.[62]

Unfortunately, physical rehabilitation is often underutilized in treating small animals with osteoarthritis, and we believe this is a mistake. Clinical evidence has shown that exercise is often as important as drug therapy or surgery, without the negative side effects or complications. Coupled with supplementation of

> To restore freedom of movement in your beloved dog or cat, exercise is the ticket!

glucosamine and chondroitin sulfate, exercise can improve flexibility and strengthen joints.

Exercise is a required component of the Arthritis Cure for Pets, regardless of the stage of the disease and the degree of disability. Of course, the specific exercises may be tailored to each animal's needs, but exercise of some sort is always beneficial. As a pet owner, you may feel sorry for a beloved companion animal that has difficulty getting up and then can only hobble around the house. It often seems as though the kindest thing to do is allow your pet to rest. That hesitant gait and difficulty in rising, however, may be due to a lack of exercise as much as the disease itself.

Why Rest Is Not Beneficial

Given the pain and discomfort often associated with osteoarthritis, it might seem that rest would improve the situation. But such is not the case. Joints that are not exercised can stiffen. In addition, the lack of exercise can lead to weight gain, a risk factor for osteoarthritis. The less activity there is, the greater the chance that muscles will atrophy, or wither, and become nearly useless.

In their natural state, animals were meant to roam about, and sufficient exercise was never an issue. Without activity, muscle and bone waste away, losing tone, strength, and flexibility. Cartilage and bone thin and soften, making them vulnerable to a variety of ailments. So even while giving an animal supplements such as glucosamine and chondroitin sulfate, it is still important to exercise.

The Benefits of Exercise

Arthritic men and women who exercise report improvement in symptoms, including increased flexibility of the affected joints, pain relief, less depression, more energy, reduced stress, and more sound sleep. Since animals with arthritis can experience the same symptoms, it stands to reason that they can also experience the same benefits.

Many human studies have also shown that regular exercise lowers the risk of dying from such common killers as heart disease and cancer. Again, the same is true for animals. Caring for your pet by making sure it exercises is one of the best things you can do. To create an appropriate therapeutic regimen, however, you may want to contact a supportive veterinarian who will work with you and your pet. Or you can use the guidelines below to create your own workout. Either way, your pet's symptoms should improve. And who knows — you just might benefit from a little more activity too!

Specific Effects of Exercise on Joints

As an animal moves, it unwittingly nourishes its joints, as motion causes synovial fluid to be squeezed in and out of the joint space. The spongy cartilage absorbs this fluid and remains moist and healthy. Synovial fluids also deliver nutrients and oxygen to joint tissue, and at the same time remove waste products, such as carbon dioxide, that accumulate from normal metabolic processes.

Cartilage, which covers the ends of the bones and makes up the bulk of the joint, has no blood supply of its own. There must be motion for vital substances that keep joints healthy to reach the cartilage tissues. When an animal spends most of its waking hours lounging and napping, very little of this health-giving exchange of substances takes place. Cartilage deterioration begins. And as the preceding chapters have explained, when there is damage to cartilage, osteoarthritis soon follows.

If you watch an arthritic animal stand up after it has been sitting or lying down for a period of time, you see what a lack of lubrication means in terms of flexibility. The animal's joints have become stiff from being sedentary, and movement is awkward.

Activity that involves impact, such as running or jumping, also strengthens bones, in turn strengthening the skeletal joints.

> **Exercise also builds strength in the muscles, tendons, and ligaments associated with joints, protecting the joint from strain and helping to keep it in its correct anatomical position. Limbs that are functioning poorly because of arthritis can be rejuvenated with exercise.**

Bones are not static rods of minerals, but rather constantly changing tissues made up of a complex of minerals and proteins. When a bone is involved in weight-bearing activity, like walking or running, nature uses this impact as a cue to build bone. Minerals are absorbed and incorporated into the skeleton. In contrast, a lack of force on bones, such as with prolonged inactivity, leads to loss of bone mass and strength. Bone lives by the old adage — use it or lose it.

Three Ways for Pets to Work Out

Ideally, an exercise program should include each of the three basic types of exercise — aerobic activity, stretching, and strength training. This is much easier than it may sound. The important thing to remember is that you need to observe your pet closely, especially if it is not accustomed to being exercised, for signs of pain, such as wincing or whining. These behaviors could be signs that the exercise is too strenuous. Excessive activity may worsen an inflamed joint. Moderation and control are the key words to keep in mind when developing an exercise program for your pet.

Aerobic Exercise

Aerobic exercise is defined as any activity that raises the heart rate and keeps it elevated for at least fifteen to twenty consecutive minutes. Aerobic exercise is essential for good health for a number of reasons. One of the most important is that it increases blood flow throughout the body, including arthritic joints, where tissues are nourished. This form of exercise relieves pain and stiffness and is also important for maintaining cardiovascular health. It's usually easy to get a dog to participate in aerobic activity. If you live in a house that has a backyard, near a park that welcomes dogs, or better yet in the country with open fields, spend twenty to thirty minutes each day outdoors with your dog, throwing a ball or a stick. If your dog is smaller, nonathletic, or simply not interested in fetching or catching, brisk walks or jogs are another option.

On the other hand, cats rarely do anything on command. Often the best way to get a cat to exercise is to let it go outside or roam an enclosed outdoor space, where it can "invent" its own activity. The more interesting the area, the better. If your cat is strictly an indoor pet, providing it with the carpeted "cat trees" of different levels may be enough to get it moving.

Don't neglect the cat's natural instinct to sharpen its claws. There are actually exercise benefits involved. Since the cat uses its claws to knead and stretch, it is working the muscles of its forelegs, shoulders, and backbone. A scratching post may do the trick, but most commercial ones, regardless of the price, are often abandoned in preference for upholstery or a tree trunk. Spritzing the scratching post with catnip spray or sprinkling it with dried catnip can help. To get your cat's attention, you could try playing hide-and-seek, which some cats love. Or tie a small object to the end of a string, then pull the object past your cat and watch it pounce, run, leap, and have a grand time while exercising and lubricating its joints.

Any toy you make for your cat should be safe for chewing and biting. Avoid using rubber bands, since cats often try to eat them. Natural materials, like rawhide or leather, are good. Your cat may have a fine time playing with a string or a ball of yarn, but it is not a good idea to leave a cat alone with them. It could become entangled or even swallow these playthings. Some cats like to chase wadded-up tin-foil balls. You can sprinkle catnip inside them — or almost any toy — to make them more attractive. Care should be taken when dogs or cats are allowed to play with toys even made of stringlike materials. The material may lodge around the tongue or in the stomach if swallowed, leading to intestinal obstructions.

Stretching Exercise

To help increase flexibility of affected joints, stretching should be performed every day. Give special attention to joints that are most sensitive or seem to be creating the most discomfort for your pet. It is also important that an animal stretch joints and muscles that are still in good condition, to keep them that way!

Although stretching is second nature for animals, you can help your pet by assisting with stretching exercises. Joints should be flexed and extended several times daily through their normal "range of motion." In other words, bend and flex the joint to the same extent that it would be used if the animal could move naturally. Gently stretch each joint for two or three minutes several times a day, until you see improvement in your pet's movements. Swimming is also a good stretching exercise for dogs — unfortunately, cats are not interested in getting wet, especially on a daily basis.

> It is important to make sure that your dog gets enough stretching exercise. It may be necessary for the dog owner to hold a treat of some sort high over the dog's head and make it stretch to reach for the treat. Cats generally stretch naturally on rising from sleep, and so do not need assistance in this respect. If your cat has trouble stretching, stroking or brushing its hair may encourage it to move.

When Alicia's twelve-year-old cat, Kiku, stopped jumping on the bed every night, she knew something was wrong. The veterinarian discovered arthritis in Kiku's hip joints, and encouraged Alicia to keep her active. At first, that seemed easier said than done. Kiku would no longer jump onto the bathroom counter to get her food or the window seat for sunning. And she could get to her favorite sleeping spot — the pillow above Alicia's head — only if Alicia picked her up and put her there.

Luckily for Kiku, Alicia found a solution, one that not only allowed Kiku to visit all her favorite haunts again but also enabled her to get some stretching and leaping activity. While sorting through items at a garage sale, Alicia found a tiny stepping stool with a needlepoint cover. At first, she simply thought it was cute. Then she realized it was just what Kiku needed. As it turned out, she was right. Alicia's two-dollar investment turned out to be a boon to her cat, which was perfectly able to hop onto the stool, and then make the short leap to the bed. Alicia positioned small boxes in front of the bathroom counter and the window seat, and before long Kiku was able to return to her favorite spots, while getting the exercise she needed.

Exercise That Strengthens

Building muscles, ligaments, and tendons provides joints with strong support, thereby taking pressure off damaged and painful joints, and transferring it to the supporting structures. An animal with well-developed muscles has less risk of injuring a joint and is less likely to develop osteoarthritis than one with poor muscle tone.

Walking, fetching, jogging, running, swimming, or controlled jumping are good ways to build strength while getting an aerobic workout. If your pet is just beginning to exercise, begin slowly, then gradually increase the duration and intensity of the workout. Watch your pet carefully and stop if you see signs of tiring, reluctance, or lameness. If symptoms are noticeably worse the next morning, the previous day's exercise was probably too intense.

A particular challenge is to make certain that an older or elderly animal has the benefit of strength-building exercise. This can be difficult if the animal has other medical problems, such as heart disease or respiratory problems, or seems to have lost interest in activity.

When his cockapoo, Tiger, reached the ripe old age of thirteen, Andy celebrated with a birthday party at the park for Tiger and several of his dog friends. But a few months later, during a particularly nasty winter, Tiger seemed to lose interest in making the six-block walk to the park. As the bad weather dragged on, Tiger took to his sheepskin-lined basket and had no interest in much of anything except sleeping.

Andy had all but given up. He traded in their long walks for brief appearances outside the apartment, where Tiger would do his business and whine to go back inside.

This state might have continued indefinitely if Andy hadn't run into another dog owner he knew from the park, who asked about Tiger. When Andy described the situation, the friend suggested he carry Tiger to the park, so the little fellow could at least visit with his old pals. The next day Andy tucked Tiger into his jacket, and they walked to the park. The first thing Andy noticed was that Tiger seemed to be enjoying being out, especially since he didn't have to walk on his own. Alert and inquisitive, he sniffed the air, took in every detail, and licked Andy's face as they neared the park.

But it wasn't until Andy set Tiger on the grass with his friends that he realized he had done the right thing. After reacquainting himself with his old pals from the birthday party days, Tiger ran around the park like he was a pup again. When he tired after a few minutes, Andy picked him up and carried him home. Although he was a little stiff the following morning, Andy took him back to the park. Again, Tiger chased his friends, then came to Andy's side when he was tired. By the time a month had passed, Tiger was strong enough to walk part of the way to the park. Best of all, his sheepskin bed wasn't the only thing he was interested in any longer.

Be Consistent

To help keep joints and tendons flexible and well lubricated, make sure your pet exercises every joint, every day, to some degree. A little daily exercise is preferable to long sessions of vigorous exercise twice a week. Start with a short exercise session, then ease into longer periods. It is better for arthritic pets to exercise three times a day for fifteen to thirty minutes than once a day for several hours.

> If exercise makes your dog's joint hot and swollen, it's very possible that the capsule of the joint or ligaments have been stretched. If so, the surrounding tissue and ligaments may be temporarily unable to support the joint. Your veterinarian can provide aids known as splints, which are similar to those worn by humans who have injured a joint. Splints help reduce stress on the joint and prevent straining or stretching the ligaments when they are vulnerable.

Water Workouts

Swimming is often prescribed for arthritic patients. It provides aerobic benefits, builds muscles, and allows joints to be rotated and stretched under non-weight-bearing conditions. The resistance of the water helps support the body and protects against sudden movements that can strain a muscle or stress a joint. In addition, swimming relaxes the muscles.

While exercising in the water, humans and animals maintain a lower heart rate, so more exercise can be tolerated. Furthermore, since swimming creates minimal stress, an animal can continue exercising even during periods when the symptoms of arthritis flare up. Swimming can also improve coordination and natural posture. In some cases this may be the only way that an arthritic animal can exercise without pain.

Swimming is an excellent exercise option for a dog with joint problems. Ponds, swimming pools, a large trough, a children's plastic wading pool, or even the bathtub can be used, depending on the size of the dog. A good swim can be the exercise equivalent of a good run. If the dog is not a swimmer and has a tendency to sink, bring a cloth or towel to place under its body like a sling. This way, your dog can paddle without panicking. The towel trick is also a good way to exercise dogs with back problems.

Rigorous vs. Moderate Exercise

Overly vigorous exercise can damage joints. If a dog or a cat has advanced osteoarthritis and is suffering from pain and inflammation, it may be more appropriate to give the animal indoor exercise, limiting runs to a hallway and letting it chase a ball around the bedroom. Many studies have documented that excessive exercise can be harmful.[63] Swiss researchers followed the medical histories of long-distance runners, bobsled riders, and healthy nonathletes. The participants were examined and X-rayed in 1973 and again in 1988, with revealing results. The runners showed the highest incidence of osteoarthritis in the hip, and the severity correlated with the speed and distance of their running fifteen years earlier. The intensity of exercise needs to be appropriate to the physiology of the animal being treated for osteoarthritis. A small, short-legged, hyperactive dog that has been trained to leap for Frisbees may have significant damage in its knee or hip joints. For these pets, swimming in the bathtub or walking are more appropriate than jogging or hiking. Meanwhile, a larger dog that has never bounced around and spends most of its time lying down could benefit from brisk walks or jogs.

The effects of excessively punishing exercise on humans and animals alike were confirmed in a review article that looked at the correlation of running and osteoarthritis. From previous studies, the researcher concluded that moderate running does not increase the risk of the disease or speed its progress in persons with normal anatomy.[64]

Tips for Therapeutic Exercise

- Aim for activities like swimming, long walks, and trotting or jogging. These provide aerobic, stretching, and strengthening exercises all at once.

- Never allow your pet to overexert. As muscles fatigue from excessive exercise, more stress is placed on the joints, leading to increased pain and more severe arthritis.

- In warm weather, be careful to avoid overheating your pet during exercise. Have plenty of water available and take frequent breaks to allow your pet to cool down.

- Range-of-motion exercises are very important, especially in the beginning of an exercise program. They promote flexible joints and muscles and encourage an early return to function. The joints should be flexed three times daily for two or three minutes each time.

- If a front leg is injured, avoid activities that require jumping down from a height. If a rear leg is affected, jumping up creates added stress on the affected limb.

- Wait two to three hours after your dog has eaten to exercise. Vigorous activity after meals could result in bloat, a life-threatening condition in which the stomach swells. A bloated stomach can become twisted. If this happens, the dog needs emergency veterinary care. Symptoms of bloat include abdominal pain, restlessness, drooling, or unsuccessful attempts to vomit or defecate.

Other Types of Arthritis

House pets and larger animals are all vulnerable to types of arthritis other than osteoarthritis, including idiopathic polyarthritis, autoimmune erosive arthritis (rheumatoid arthritis), systemic lupus erythematosus, and Lyme disease. These conditions may occur on their own or be coupled with osteoarthritis. If the latter is the case, symptoms are compounded and the severity of the diseases increases dramatically. These forms of arthritis have been widely researched in humans, and much of what we know about them today applies to animal patients as well. Let's take a look at each specific condition. It is important to be familiar with the signs and symptoms of these different health problems so that you can spot them if your pet becomes ill. The more information that you can provide your veterinarian, the more accurate the diagnosis and the more beneficial the treatment.

Idiopathic Polyarthritis (IP)

Idiopathic polyarthritis is the most common form of immune-mediated (caused by the body's own immune system), nonerosive (no erosion of joint cartilage) polyarthritis in dogs. It affects both large and small breeds, but is more common in larger dogs. It is not usually seen in cats. Fortunately, the disease is not known to be hereditary. Breeds that are most usually affected include German shepherds, Doberman pinschers, retrievers, spaniels, pointers, toy poodles, Lhaso apsos, Yorkshire terriers, and Chihuahuas.

Causes of idiopathic polyarthritis: The cause of IP is unknown; however, it is associated with an overreactive immune system.

Symptoms and signs of idiopathic polyarthritis: Animals with this condition show lameness in one or more limbs. The lameness is not associated with trauma and may shift from leg to leg. Other symptoms include stiffness of gait, fever, joint swelling, lethargy, anorexia, and pain in one or more of the joints. IP can affect all joints but is most commonly seen in the carpus (wrist) and tarsus (ankle). Treatment with steroids is usually successful.

Autoimmune Erosive Arthritis (EA)

EA is a potentially debilitating disease, similar to rheumatoid arthritis in people. As a result of some change in the immune system, the animal's own cells begin to attack themselves and create antibodies against its own cells. This phenomenon is known as autoimmune disease and leads to intense inflammation and joint disease.

Fortunately this type of arthritis is rarely seen in dogs. When it does occur, the animal experiences chronic, progressive inflammation throughout the body, usually on both sides of a given area. In other words, two ankles or two knees will become inflamed simultaneously. Joints can erode and become deformed, disabling the animal. Small breeds, such as the miniature poodle and Pekinese, are most commonly affected.

Causes of autoimmune erosive arthritis: The causes of EA are not known. Some experts speculate that a virus or bacteria may be the source. Another theory is that the condition develops after exposure to heavy metals, such as lead. Genetics appears to play a role, since the disease tends to run in families and is much more common in females. However, these theories are currently supported by only anecdotal evidence.

Symptoms and signs of autoimmune erosive arthritis: In the early stages the first obvious sign is inflammation, which might be severe and can escalate into synovitis, an inflammation of the lining of the joint. An animal with EA has aching joints, and there is a noticeable stiffness in its movements. Although any joint is vulnerable, in humans the fingers, wrists, and feet are usually affected first. In dogs the disease attacks equivalent joints, which are toes, wrists (carpi), and ankles (tarsi). Obviously, autoimmune erosive arthritis coupled with osteoarthritis seriously compromises any animal's health.

The progression of EA is so slow that it may be difficult to tell when the ailment first began. In fact, general fatigue or weakness may appear even before pain becomes noticeable. In rare cases there is rapid onset, with dramatic symptoms such as swollen, painful joints showing up literally overnight.

To make an accurate diagnosis, a veterinarian may have to observe the ailing animal intermittently over a period of months. Many human patients recover spontaneously during this period because there are varying degrees of the disease, as well as temporary forms. Like those suffering from osteoarthritis, animals with EA have stiff joints in the morning, and staying in a fixed position for long periods of time can also cause discomfort.

In the later stages of the disease, symptoms become more severe. There may be damage to cartilage, ligaments, tendons, and even bone. If joints appear out of alignment, tendons and ligaments may have been affected. Skeletal deformities are sometimes seen in the limbs and other areas. And if the deterioration caused by EA progresses, an animal's range of motion becomes limited, and it will be unable to perform routine, familiar tasks, such as nudging a door open to leave a room. Eventually walking may become difficult, as the knees and hips become involved.

Systemic Lupus Erythematosus

Another autoimmune disease, lupus attacks and inflames connective tissue, the fibrous and fatty tissues throughout the body. The immune system produces abnormal substances called "antinuclear" antibodies, which damage tissues in the joints, especially those in the fingers, wrists, and knees. The exact causes of lupus remain a mystery.

Symptoms and signs of lupus: Symptoms include joint pain, inflammation, and stiffness. Lupus can also affect the lymph nodes, kidneys, nervous system, lungs, and the heart, as well as the skin. In humans a sign of this disease is a butterfly-shaped rash that spreads across the bridge of the nose and cheeks. Exposure to sunlight usually makes the rash worse.

Symptoms in people are frequently moderate, and patients are able to perform most tasks, if not all their normal functions. Others have such slight symptoms that the disease is barely noticeable. Lupus can cause serious illness, though. Obviously, an animal with lupus and osteoarthritis is going to experience considerable physical difficulties.

Treatment of lupus: Rest is recommended during the active phases of the disease. Otherwise, exercise is advised, since it increases joint mobility. Medications include aspirin, NSAIDs, and antimalarial drugs for active attacks.

Lyme Disease

This disease was first recognized in humans in Europe during the early 1900s. Subsequently, it has also been reported in Russia, China, Australia, Africa, and Japan. In America the ailment acquired the name Lyme disease in 1975, when it was found to cause arthritis in children in Old Lyme, Connecticut. It is now prevalent in southern New England, the Middle Atlantic states, Georgia, Wisconsin, and California.

Cause of lyme disease: After much research, a bacterium known as *Borrelia burgdorferi* was identified as the cause of Lyme disease. Ticks carry this bacterium and transmit it to animals when they feed on their blood. The tick must remain attached to the animal for twenty-four to seventy-two hours in order for the disease to be transmitted. Not all ticks carry the disease. In the United States, deer ticks are primarily responsible, although in the West, western black-legged ticks are the carriers. Cases of Lyme disease usually occur in a few highly affected areas where the bacterium is prevalent. Since an indoor dog or cat is normally never exposed to ticks, there is little chance of their developing the disease.

Symptoms and signs of Lyme disease: In humans Lyme disease causes joint problems as well as fatigue, rash, fevers and chills, backache, and headache. In advanced stages the symptoms can include chronic arthritis and muscle pain, as well as problems with the nervous system. In contrast, the symptoms of the disease are relatively mild in dogs. If a dog does develop the disease, symptoms include fever and hot, painful, stiff joints, especially in the joints comparable to the wrist in humans. Depression is another symptom.

In cats the first symptoms are fatigue, lethargy, fever, and a loss of appetite. Felines, however, are more resistant to infection than dogs. During a study conducted at Texas A & M University, researchers infected cats with the Lyme disease bacterium. Although there was evidence of antibodies, along with tissue and organ damage, the cats were symptom-free. The same has been found to be true for mice and the deer that carry the disease.

Lyme disease would increase complications for an animal with osteoarthritis. There is, however, a Lyme disease vaccine available for pets now. If your veterinarian feels it is appropriate, you may want to have your pet inoculated.

Treatment of Lyme disease: About 15 percent of dogs treated with antibiotics such as tetracycline and doxycycline will remain chronically ill, but the majority enjoy permanent recovery. A raw diet, which is recommended for general animal health and support of the immune system, is also helpful for Lyme disease, as are vitamin C and trace minerals.

Contracting any of the above diseases with or without osteoarthritis can bring on a complex array of symptoms. Although it was developed to treat osteoarthritis, the Arthritis Cure for Pets can help with these other forms of arthritis too, since a good diet supports the immune system, exercise strengthens joints, and glucosamine and chondroitin sulfate can work to stop the progression of joint deterioration.

Your Aging Pet

For many people the most difficult aspect of owning a pet is watching it grow old. No one likes to think about saying good-bye to a dear and trusted friend — which is exactly what a pet is. But since there is no alternative, the best approach is to make an animal's last years as comfortable and pleasant as possible. If you follow the guidelines in the Arthritis Cure for Pets, rest assured that you are doing everything possible for your pet's joint health. With a little extra knowledge about how animals age, though, you can easily fulfill your older pet's needs so that the later years take as small a toll as possible.

A New Look at Aging

In our society there is tremendous resistance to growing old. But with the bulk of the population doing just that, scientists are actively searching for that elusive "fountain of youth" that will allow us to remain in our prime indefinitely. Meanwhile, we are taking advantage of anti-aging discoveries that have been made along the way. Today the average human life span has almost doubled from what it was at the turn of the century, and some longevity experts predict that in the baby-boom generation, living to be a hundred will be commonplace.

The real issue, many experts now say, is not how long we are able to live but how well. No doubt you have seen older people who were just as active and alert as a person many decades younger. And, of course, most of us are familiar with the opposite scenario, those elderly individuals who seem to be barely alive. Obviously, when we talk about living longer, we are also hoping there will not just be more years in our lives but more life in our years as well.

Like people, pets are living longer than ever. But are they living better? Certainly a cherished dog or cat that doesn't have to fend for itself in the wild has an advantage over its ancestors. And although cancer is common in animals, pets are far less likely than people to die from such everyday ailments as heart attacks or strokes. For animals the aging process is a gradual decline. The good news is that the old standard of one dog year being the equivalent of seven human years has been updated. Now one dog year is the same as only five and a half human years, meaning dogs are truly living longer than before.

Still, dogs and cats are generally considered to be "middle-age" or "seniors" by the time they are eight or nine years old. About then, pet owners may notice only that their animals are slowing down a little. But the more important changes are taking place internally, on the cellular level. During the later years, as the body's ability to repair itself slows, animals become more vulnerable to injury and illness. One or more of the systems that perform specific bodily functions — such as cardiovascular, digestive, or sensory — may become less efficient. Because these systems are interrelated, a shortcoming in one affects the others.

So, for example, when an older dog's digestive system has trouble, it will not be able to provide the rest of the body with the nutrients it needs to function at a peak level. Or when an elderly cat spends nearly all its time sleeping, its body is not getting the oxygen it needs, and muscles and bones may wither as well. As the effects of these changes compound, daily living becomes more difficult for the pet.

Is there any way to slow or stop these changes from occurring in the first place? That question is difficult to answer, because no one yet knows exactly why the aging process takes place. Basically, there are four theories as to why we grow older — genetic, wear-and-tear, free-radical, and neuroendocrine. In order to understand how to avoid aging, we first need to understand what it is — or at least, what it might be.

Genetics: All living things contain DNA, a chemical substance that is considered "life's blueprint." DNA determines everything from the color of our hair and eyes to how long we will live. DNA is inherited from parents, so some congenital health conditions are the result of what previous generations pass on to us. DNA can also be damaged, though, by chemicals, radiation, and viruses. In just a few years the Human Genome Project will have completely mapped the genes in the human body. Then it will be only a matter of time before it becomes possible to replace defective genes and "cure" hereditary ailments.

Of course, this type of operation will be costly, and reserved for life-threatening illness, at least in the beginning. Will a similar map eventually become available for animals? No doubt it will, but in the meantime, you can actively improve the situation by making certain your pet gets a healthy diet, enriched with vitamins, minerals, and herbs that provide the building blocks of DNA. This advice does not apply only to those of us with older pets. A young animal that has the benefit of a top-quality diet may never need to face many of the problems associated with age-related decline.

Wear-and-tear: "Use it or lose it" works up to a point, says the wear-and-tear theory of aging. But overusing it and abusing it can hasten the aging process. According to this approach, the best way to correct the situation is with a strong immune system, which means support from the right diet and appropriate exercise.

Free radicals: As shown in Chapter 6, an abundance of free radicals in the body can cause everything from disease to aging. After all, if the oxidation process that produces these scavengers can rust metal, imagine what it can do to a living organism. The solution: load up on recognized antioxidants to combat the free radicals.

Neuroendocrine: As we grow older, our bodies produce fewer good hormones than in earlier years. This theory claims that it is the lack of such hormones that causes certain bodily functions to slow down. Again, supplements are the best way to restore hormone levels to those of youth.

•   •   •

Of these theories, genetics is the most widely accepted (although that doesn't mean the others aren't valid). Not surprisingly, the changes that occur in humans as a result of the biological clock ticking away in our genes is similar to what happens to animals. According to one study at the University of California, by the time a dog is sixteen years old, it is likely to experience such typically human "symptoms" of old age as disorientation, difficulty maintaining normal sleep patterns, and a lessened interest in social activities.

How Aging Affects Pets

Knowing the role that genes play helps us understand the common events taking place as our pets age. As pets mature, the various body systems change.

Metabolic system: At about age six or seven, a dog's or cat's metabolism slows. This means your pet does not need quite as much food as it did when it was younger, and you can avoid excess weight gain later by cutting back the amount you feed now by 20 to 40 percent. This is especially important since a slower metabolism will gradually rob your pet of muscle mass, while increasing fat stores.

A slower metabolism also means that healing takes longer, so it is wise to be especially vigilant about any injuries that occur in later years. A pet's sensitivity to temperature may also increase, and extremes of hot and cold affect it much more than in earlier years. A pet may lose its ability to recognize when it is thirsty, which could result in dehydration. Making certain plenty of fresh water is available and avoiding activities that overheat your older pet are two ways to deal with this problem.

As for diet and supplements, the metabolism responds well to complex carbohydrates and fiber (found in vegetables and grains), foods containing omega-3 fatty acids (fish, flaxseed and flaxseed oil, borage and evening primrose oils), vitamins A, B-complex, C, D, E, and K, and beta-carotene and flavonoids.

Cardiovascular system: Although pets do not have to worry about heart disease or cholesterol levels, their cardiovascular systems are affected by age. The primary change is a reduction in efficiency. Since the cardiovascular system includes not only the heart but the arteries, veins, and capillaries, less efficiency translates into deficient nutrients, oxygen, and other substances required for optimal functioning. The reduced amount of oxygen relayed to the brain is, in fact, the cause of senility many pets, especially dogs, experience as they grow older. Regular, moderate exercise is the best way to keep the cardiovascular system in working order.

Digestive system: A fully functioning digestive system is essential for the rest of the body's operations, since it is responsible for breaking down food into chemical substances that can be used for energy and nourishment of tissues. In older pets this system is prone to a host of problems, including everything from inefficient muscles (which make it harder to move food throughout the body) to dental diseases that affect how well a pet eats, as well as what it will eat.

Since the digestive system is in many ways the key to overall health, we cannot stress enough the importance of a nutritious diet, particularly for the pet who is taking medicine or supplements to alleviate osteoarthritis. If the stomach can't digest food properly, it may have trouble with supplements too. That is why every effort should be made to feed older pets the best possible food.

Antioxidants are very helpful in protecting the liver from free radicals. Lecithin is available in health food stores, and milk thistle, an herb found in health food stores, is often recommended for humans with liver damage. For a dog that weighs twenty pounds, a daily dose of 25 mg of milk thistle is ideal. (Use that figure as a guideline for other weights.) Antioxidant enzymes like superoxide dismutase (SOD) and catalase are other good additions to an aging pet's diet. Many veterinarians routinely stock these supplements.

Respiratory system: The changes that occur with aging can reduce an animal's respiratory system functions by half. In other words, an older pet is able to take in only about half as much oxygen as it did in its youth. As an animal grows older, there are fewer of the tiny, hairlike parts of the respiratory system called *cilia,* which clear mucus and other substances from the airways. Meanwhile, the *alveoli,* small air sacs in the lungs, become less efficient, and the amount of fibrous tissue in the lungs increases, further reducing efficiency. In addition to these physical changes, external factors also play a major role in a pet's breathing ability. Pollution, including smog and cigarette smoke, have a tremendous effect on lung capacity.

With reduced supplies of oxygen throughout the body, the blood is deprived of this essential cleansing substance, the cardiovascular system must work overtime, and brain cells suffer. Moderate exercise several times a day can help increase the oxygen supply, while antioxidants battle the effects of pollution and other toxins.

Urinary system: Although we think of the urinary system (bladder, urethra, ureter, and kidneys) only as a means of elimination, it is actually much more. The urinary system removes wastes and toxins along with urine, and controls the electrolyte and acidic balance of fluids in the body. As an animal grows older, the kidneys diminish in size and lose some of their ability to cleanse the blood, so toxins can accumulate in the body. Nutritional supplements, exercise, herbs, and a watchful eye on salt intake can go a long way toward maintaining a healthy urinary tract.

Immune system: This all-important system is made up of a number of elements, including the lymph system, spleen, bone marrow, and thymus gland. White blood cells called leukocytes are produced in the bone marrow and then distributed throughout the body. These cells are responsible for defending the body against invaders, and they accomplish the task by releasing antibodies, protein "warriors" that destroy foreign matter, such as bacteria and viruses. When the immune system is functioning at its peak, it repels enemies easily. As a pet ages, though, its immune system slows, and functions are compromised. Consequently, an older pet is vulnerable to infections and a variety of other illnesses. In some cases the immune system goes seriously awry, releasing antibodies against its own tissues. Autoimmune erosive arthritis is one such autoimmune disease. Keeping the immune system strong requires a good diet and supplements, including vitamins A, B-complex, C, and E, as well as selenium, zinc, and the essential fatty acids, all of which are discussed in Chapter 6. Herbs such as astralagus, aloe vera, garlic, ginseng, goldenseal, echinacea, and kelp have also been recommended by some veterinarians. Giving these supplements once a week is fine. A twenty-pound dog would receive one-fifth of the human dose. So, for example, if you wanted to give a twenty-pound dog an herb with the recommended human dose of five capsules, give it one capsule. If the dog weighs forty pounds, the correct dosage is two capsules.

Musculoskeletal system: Earlier in this book, we looked at the musculoskeletal system in detail. The bones and muscles in an animal's body work in conjunction to allow movement. Strong muscles provide support for joints and bones, and enable an animal to move as nature intended. Loss of muscle mass and bone density occur during aging, though, making even simple movements challenging. The weaker a pet becomes, the less active it is likely to be and the worse the bones and muscles fare. Complicating matters further, age-related deterioration in the cartilage tissue in the joints can lead to osteoarthritis, an even more painful situation. As we know, however, keeping cartilage healthy through the use of glucosamine and chondroitin sulfate supplements is an important key to avoiding this type of degeneration.

Improving Quality of Life for an Aging Pet

By following a few simple guidelines, you can make life better for your pet as it grows older.

- The easiest and most obvious thing one can do is to pay attention to a pet in its later years. Too often, we take our animal companions for granted, assuming that they will always be there. But spending a little time each week *purposefully* in contact with your pet can provide early clues to problems. As you pet your dog or cat, for example, take note of how its fur feels, whether its skin is dry, and if there are any bumps or irregularities on the skin. Check its eyes for any filming, mucus, or tearing. Make sure that its nose is free of discharge, the ears are clean, odorless, and pale pink inside and that the gums are moist and pink. (White or very pale gums can be a symptom of serious illness, by the way. If you find this condition in your pet, call your veterinarian immediately.) Also, run your hands down your pet's legs, across its back and stomach and chest. If you notice any particularly sensitive areas, make note of them and discuss them with your veterinarian at the next visit — or sooner, if they seem very tender.

This entire process should take no more than five or ten minutes but can make a tremendous difference. Getting to know how your pet feels and looks when it is healthy gives you a "baseline" for later comparisons.

- Watch your pet's diet and its impact on weight. Cut back the amount at each feeding if your pet gains weight. One way to help a pet make the adjustment to decreased amounts of food is by feeding several small meals a day instead of only one large one. This practice is especially helpful for an older animal's less-efficient digestive system.
- Apply the same approach to exercise. Instead of trying to accomplish a week's worth of activity in one day, break up exercise into brief intervals throughout the day. This allows for a recovery period and places less stress on joints. It is also a good way for dogs to avoid the housebreaking "accidents" that sometimes occur with aging.
- Provide your pet with a warm, clean, dry sleeping spot. It could be nothing more than a couple of old blankets folded into a pad, or a large pillow. In older dogs, stress reactions last longer, so they tend to overproduce harmful, stress-related hormones known as glucocorticoids. By giving a pet a place to sleep comfortably, it is better able to relax, which in turn can help reduce overall stress.
- Take a few minutes each day to groom your pet. Older cats sometimes lose the flexibility required to do a thorough job, and dogs too can find it difficult to accomplish all the grooming necessary. Best of all, brushing your pet's coat is an easy way to boost circulation, benefit the entire body, and relax your pet.
- Schedule regular trips to the veterinarian twice a year. These examinations can run the gamut, from a complete physical

(including ultrasound, X rays, blood and urine tests) to a simple blood test and hands-on exam. The blood test, or blood panel, usually costs less than $100 and takes only a few seconds but can provide the veterinarian with a wealth of information on your pet's bodily functions and allow him or her to catch imbalances before they become major illnesses. Proper dental care is also important since infected gums and teeth are a common cause for bacteria entering the bloodstream.

• Make a point of subscribing to at least one reputable pet magazine, and check for new books on pet health in your bookstore. Staying abreast of new developments is a great way to help your pet through the aging process. The field of medicine is changing so rapidly that new treatments for "incurable" diseases are becoming commonplace. Only a few years ago arthritis was considered a chronic disease that one learned to live with. Today, with glucosamine and chondroitin sulfate sweeping the nation, that is no longer true.

For a pet owner, helping a pet age gracefully means taking care of its health at every age. The sooner you begin feeding your dog or cat quality foods, exercising it, and providing it with supplements, the later the aging process begins. Someday there may be a "miracle drug" or magic potion to ward off the infirmities we now accept as part of growing older. Until that time, giving your pet the advantages of our newfound knowledge of aging gives you both more quality time together — and who could ask for more?

Notes

Chapter 1

1. M. J. Friedrich, "Steps Toward Understanding, Alleviating Osteoarthritis Will Help Aging Population," *Journal of the American Medical Association* 282, no. 11 (1999): 1023–25.
2. J. A. Buckwalter and N. E. Lane, "Athletics and Osteoarthritis," *American Journal of Sports Medicine* 25, no. 6 (1997): 873–81.
3. J. A. Buckwalter and H. J. Mankin, "Articular Cartilage: Degeneration and Osteoarthritis, Repair, Regeneration, and Transplantation," *Instructional Course Lectures* 47 (1998): 487–504.
4. P. Gross and B. Marti, "Sports Activity and Risk of Arthrosis," *Schweizerische Medizinishe Wochenschrift* 127, no. 23 (1997): 967–77.
5. M. Arican, S. D. Carter, D. Bennett, G. Ross, and S. Ayad, "Increased Metabolism of Collagen VI in Canine Osteoarthritis," *J ComP Path* 114 (1996): 249–56.
6. J. R. Matyas et al., "Major Role of Collagen IIB in the Elevation of Total Type II Procollagen Messenger RNA in the Hypertrophic Phase of Experimental Osteoarthritis," *Arthritis & Rheumatism* 40, no. 6 (1997): 1046–49.

Chapter 2

7. D. C. Richardson et al., "Nutritional Management of Osteoarthritis," *Veterinary Clinics of North America* 27, no. 4 (1997): 883–911.
8. E. M. Hardie, "Management of osteoarthritis in cats," ibid.: 945–53.
9. D. Bennett, "Osteoarthritis — its classification, pathogenesis and clinical relevance," *Voor Diergeneeskunde* 118, supplement (1993): 19S.

10. Stacy Ann Thomas, "Free Weight Checks Stick to the Ribs," *Dallas Morning News,* June 8, 1997, p. 40A.

11. D. Bennett and C. May, "Joint Diseases of Dogs and Cats," in S. J. Ettinger and E. C. Feldman, eds., *Textbook of Small Animal Medicine,* 4th ed. (Philadelphia: W. B. Saunders, 1995), pp. 2032–77.

12. M. S. Gottlieb, "Conservative management of spinal osteoarthritis with glucosamine sulfate and chiropractic treatment," *Journal of Manipulative Physiological Therapy* 20, no. 6 (1997): 400–14.

13. S. A. Martinez, "Congenital conditions that lead to osteoarthritis in the dog," *Veterinary Clinics of North America: Small Animal Practice* 27, no. 4 (1997): 735–58.

14. Richardson, loc. cit.

15. S. A. Martinez et al., "Acquired conditions that lead to osteoarthritis in the dog," *Veterinary Clinics of North America: Small Animal Practice* 27, no. 4 (1997): 759–75.

16. Hardie, loc. cit.

17. C. C. Nolte-Ernsting et al., "The MRT of osteophytosis in experimental gonarthrosis," *Rofo Fortschr Geb Rontgenstr Neuen Bildgeb Verfahr* 163, no. 5 (1995): 430–36.

18. E. Strand et al., "Intra-articular pressure, elastance and range of motion in healthy and injured racehorses' metacarpophalangeal joints," *Equine Veterinary Journal* 30, no. 6 (1998): 520–27.

19. M. P. Brown et al., "Changes in sulfation patterns of chondroitin sulfate in equine articular cartilage and synovial fluid in response to aging and osteoarthritis," *American Journal of Veterinary Research* 59, no. 6 (1998): 786–91.

20. Sherry Joe Crosby, "With Age, How Do the Animals Fare? Scientific Adventures Aid Zoos' Geriatric Gentry," *Dallas Morning News,* April 6, 1997, p. 9A.

Chapter 3

21. D. Hulse, "Treatment Methods for Pain in the Osteoarthritic Patient," *Veterinary Clinics of North America: Small Animal Practice* 28, no. 2 (1998): 361–75.

22. Ibid.

23. E. M. Hardie, "Management of Osteoarthritis in Cats," *Veterinary Clinics of North America: Small Animal Practice* 27, no. 4 (1997): 945–53.

24. Sherine E. Gabriel and Judith L. Wagner, "Costs and Effectiveness of Nonsteroidal Anti-Inflammatory Drugs: The Importance of Reducing Side Effects." *Arthritis Care and Research* 10, no. 1 (1997): 56–63.

Chapter 4

25. L. Lippiello et al., "Beneficial Effect of Cartilage Disease-Modifying Agents Tested in Chondrocyte Cultures and a Rabbit Instability Model of Osteoarthrosis," draft abstract presented to the American College of Rheumatology, Sixty-third Annual Scientific Meeting, November 1999.

26. "Study Indicates Efficacy of Glucosamine and Chondroitin Sulfate for OA Symptoms," *Orthopedics Today* 19, no. 1 (1999): 1–2; A. K. Das, J. Eitel, and T. A. Hammad, "Efficacy of a New Class of Agents (Glucosamine Hydrochloride and Chondroitin Sulfate) in the Treatment of Osteoarthritis of the Knee," American Association of Hip and Knee Surgeons, Eighth Annual Meeting, Dallas, Texas, November 1998, p. 49; paper no. 180, American Academy of Orthopedic Surgeons, Sixty-sixth Annual Meeting, Anaheim, California, February 1998.

27. Alan F. Philippi, Christopher T. Leffler, et al., "Glucosamine, Chondroitin, and Manganese Ascorbate for Degenerative Joint Disease of the Knee or Low Back: A Randomized, Double-Blind, Placebo-Controlled Pilot Study," *Military Medicine* 164 (February 1999): 85–91.

28. M. J. Tapadinhas, I. C. Rivera, and A. A. Bignamini, "Oral Glucosamine Sulphate in the Management of Arthrosis: Report on a Multicentre Open Investigation in Portugal," *Pharmatherapeutica* 3, no. 3 (1982): 157–68.

29. A. L. Vaz, "Double-blind Clinical Evaluation of the Relative Efficacy of Ibuprofen and Glucosamine Sulphate in the Management of Osteoarthrosis of the Knee in Out-patients," *Current Medical Research and Opinion* 8, no. 3 (1982): 145–49.

30. H. J. Fassbender et al., "Glucosamine Sulfate Compared to Ibuprofen in Osteoarthritis of the Knee," *Osteoarthritis and Cartilage* 2, no. 1 (1994): 61–69.

31. A. Dovanti, A. A. Bignamini, and A. L. Rovati, "Therapeutic Activity of Oral Glucosamine Sulphate in Osteoarthrosis: A Placebo-Controlled Double-Blind Investigation," *Clinical Therapeutics* 3, no. 4 (1980): 266–72.

32. B. Mazieres et al., "Le Chondroitin Sulfate Dayns le Traitement de la Gonarthrose et de la Coxarthrose," *Rev. Rheum. Mal Osteoartic* 59, nos. 7–8 (1992): 466–72.

33. V. R. Pipitone, "Chondroprotection with Chondroitin Sulfate," *Drugs in Experimental and Clinical Research* 17, no. 1 (1991): 3–7.

34. M. J. Glade, "Polysulfated Glycosaminoglycan Accelerates Net Synthesis of Collagen and Glycosaminoglycans by Arthritic Equine Cartilage Tissue and Chondrocytes," *American Veterinary Journal Review* 51 (1990): 779.

35. R. Reid Hanson et al., "Oral Treatment with a Glucosamine–Chondroitin Sulfate Compound for Degenerative Joint Disease in Horses: 25 Cases," *Equine Practice* 19, no. 9 (1997): 16–22.

36. R. Reid Hanson et al., "Evaluation of the Clinical Efficacy of Cosequin in the Treatment of Navicular Syndrome — A Double-Blinded Placebo-Controlled Randomized Clinical Trial," Veterinary Orthopedic Society, Twenty-fifth Annual Conference, February 1998, p. 63.

37. D. Gross, "Orale Chondroitinsulfatmedikation zur behandlung von arthrosen." *Rheumatologie* 33 (1983): 4238–44.

38. R. W. Moskowitz, "The Relevance of Animal Models in Osteoarthritis," Scandinavian *Journal of Rheumatology* 81, supplement (1990): 21–23.

39. D. S. Hulse, D. Hart, M. Slatter, and B. S. Beale, "The Effect of Cosequin in Cranial Cruciate Deficient and Reconstructed Stifle Joints in Dogs," Veterinary Orthopedic Society, Twenty-fifth Annual Conference, February 1998, p. 64.

40. L. Lippiello et al., "Cartilage Stimulatory and Antiproteolytic Activity Is Present in Sera of Dogs Treated with a Chondroprotective Agent," *Canine Practice* 24 (1999): 18–19.

41. P. S. McNamara, S. C. Barr, and H. N. Erb, "Haematological, Haemostatic and Biochemical Effects in Cats Receiving an Oral Chondroprotective Agent for 30 Days," clinical research abstract presented at the Forty-second British Small Animal Veterinary Association Congress, April 8–11, 1999, p. 283.

42. P. S. McNamara, S. C. Barr, and H. N. Erb, "Haematological, Haemostatic and Biochemical Effects in Dogs Receiving an Oral Chondroprotective Agent for 30 Days." *American Journal of Veterinary Research,* 57, no. 9 (1996): 1390–94.

43. M. Anderson and M. Slater, "Evaluation of Clinical Efficacy of an Oral Glucosamine–Chondroitin Sulfate Compound: Survey of Veterinary Practices in the United States," in *Proceedings of the Seventh Annual American College of Veterinary Surgeons Symposium,* October 1997.

Chapter 6

44. T. E. McAlindon et al., "Do Antioxidant Micronutrients Protect Against the Development and Progression of Knee Osteoarthritis?" *Arthritis and Rheumatology* 39, no. 1 (1996): 648–56.

45. J. A. Impellizeri, R. E. Lau, and F. A. Azzara, "Fourteen-Week Clinical Evaluation of Oral Antioxidant as a Treatment for Osteoarthritis Secondary to Canine Hip Dysplasia," *Veterinary Quarterly* 20, supplement no. 10 (1998): S107–08.

46. E. R. Schwartz, "The Modulation of Osteoarthritic Development by Vitamins C and E," *Int. Journal of Vitamins and Nutritional Research* 26 (1984): 141–46.

47. "Do Antioxidant Nutrients Protect Against the Development and Progression of Knee Osteoarthritis?" *Arthritis & Rheumatism* 39, no. 4 (1996).

48. A. P. Prins et al., "Effect of Purified Growth Factors on Rabbit Articular Chondrocytes in Monolayer Culture," *Arthritis & Rheumatism* 25, no. 10 (1982): 1228–32.

49. C. J. Bates, "Proline and Hydroxyproline Excretion and Vitamin C Status in Elderly Human Subjects," *Clinical Science and Molecular Medicine* 52 (1977): 535–43.

50. Schwartz, loc. cit.

Notes

Chapter 7

51. P. G. Mass'e et al., "Loss of Decorin from the Surface Zone of Articular Cartilage in a Chick Model of Osteoarthritis," *Acta Histochemica* 99, no. 4 (1997): 431–44.

52. P. G. Mass'e et al., "A Cartilage Matrix Deficiency Experimentally Induced by Vitamin B$_6$ Deficiency," *Proceedings of the Society for Experimental Biology and Medicine* 217, no. 1 (1998): 97–103.

53. J. Badurksi et al., "Comparative Analysis of Three Treatment Regimens for Treating Gonarthritis with Calcitonin, Naproxen and Flavonoids Based on EULAR Criteria and Visual Analogue Scale (VAS)," *Pol Tyg Led* 50, nos. 44–47 (1995): 37–40.

54. D. C. Richardson et al., "Nutritional Management of Osteoarthritis," *Veterinary Clinics of North America: Small Animal Practice* 27, no. 4 (1997): 883–911.

55. R. D. Kealy et al., "Five-Year Longitudinal Study on Limited Food Consumption and Development of Osteoarthritis in Coxofemoral Joints in Dogs," *Journal of the American Veterinary Medical Association* 210 (1997): 222–25.

56. C. S. Carlson et al., "Osteoarthritis in Cynomolgus Macaques. III: Effects of Age, Gender, and Subchondral Bone Thickness on the Severity of Disease," *Journal of Bone and Mineral Research* 11, no. 9 (1996): 1209–17.

Chapter 8

57. L. W. Whitehouse, M. Znamirouska, and C. J. Paul, "Devil's Claw (*Harpagophytum procumbens*): No Evidence for Anti-Inflammatory Activity in the Treatment of Arthritic Disease," *Canadian Medical Association Journal* 129 (1983): 249–51.

58. C. D. Seaborn and F. H. Nielsen, "Silicon: A Nutritional Beneficence for Bones, Brains and Blood Vessels?" *Nutrition Today* 26 (1993): 190–97.

59. C. Takeshige and M. Sato, "Comparison of Pain Relief Mechanisms Between Needling to the Muscle, Static Magnetic Field, External Qigong and Needling to the Acupuncture Point," *Acupuncture and Electro-Therapeutics Research* 21, no. 2 (1996): 119–31.

60. C. Vallbona et al., "Response of Pain to Static Magnet Fields in Post-Polio Patients: A Double-Blind Pilot Study," *Archives of Physical Medicine and Rehabilitation* (November 1997): 1200–03.
61. A. Weinberger, A. Nyska, and S. Giler, "Treatment of Experimental Inflammatory Synovitis with Continuous Magnetic Field," *Israel Journal of Medical Science* 32, no. 12 (1966): 1197–1201.

Chapter 9
62. D. Hulse, "Treatment Methods of Pain in the Osteoarthritic Patient," *Veterinary Clinics of North America: Small Animal Practice* 28, no. 2 (1998): 361–75; D. L. Millis and D. Levine, "The Role of Exercise and Physical Modalities in the Treatment of Osteoarthritis," *Veterinary Clinics of North America: Small Animal Practice* 27, no. 4 (1997): 913–30.
63. C. B. Little et al., "The Effect of Strenuous Versus Moderate Exercise on the Metabolism of Proteoglycans in Articular Cartilage from Different Weight-Bearing Regions of the Equine Third Carpal Bone," *Osteoarthritis Cartilage* 5, no. 3: 161–72.
64. D. D. Lahr, "Does Running Exercise Cause Osteoarthritis?" *MD Medical Journal* 45, no. 8 (1996): 641–44.

Index